Recovery

Exercises

For Christians

Book Three

Ken Gross

i

This page intentionally left blank.

Recovery Exercises for Christians

Book Three

50 Written Exercises

Based on Scriptural Principles

Shown in the Life Stories

Of Bible Characters

Thank you Kathy Trout, my friend, co-worker in helping

others and editor of this book.

Scripture quotations are from the ESV® Bible (The Holy Bible, English Standard Version®), copyright 2001 by Crossway, a publishing ministry of Good News Publishers. Used by permission. All rights reserved.

Notice – This book of written exercises is designed to be used by those in some form of recovery program and under the guidance of a sponsor, mentor, coach or counselor. It is written with the understanding that the publisher and author are not engaged in rendering any form of professional services. The exercises provided in this book are meant to be used by an individual or a group for study purposes, and they are not in any way designed to be a substitute for one-to-one professional therapy if such help is necessary.

About the Author

Ken was born in the UK, and at age three developed tuberculosis resulting in him being taken by his family to a sanitarium for treatment. This action of abandonment, although it saved his life, set him on a path that contained many struggles, and eventually led to recovery in his own life.

Before he got there, recovery, he obtained an undergraduate degree with a joint major in Chemistry and Physics from the University of London and an MBA from the University of Oklahoma. He spent some time working in the water industry in the UK, then the oil industry in Saudi Arabia and finally in the financial services industry here in the US.

In 2009 God gave him the vision for a new style of recovery ministry and he became the founding director of Merimnao (merimnao.org) which he still runs to this day. He also wrote and published three recovery oriented books, the "Emotional Prison" series. The three book series covers how emotions trap us; looks at the major emotional prisons that exist, such as religion, false intimacy and perfectionism; and how to become free of the prisons, or healed. These books are available through Merimnao or on amazon.com, including a kindle version.

Ken is available at director@merimnao.org for those that may wish to speak with him, request him to train group leaders in Christian recovery leadership or request him to speak at retreats.

Table of Contents

Recommendations

For Sponsors, Mentors, Coaches, Pastors or Counselors

We recommend that those who are guiding others through recovery programs, a disciplined plan of spiritual formation, Christian lifestyle coaching or personal therapy use these exercises as an adjunct part of their work.

Every exercise is designed for the individual doing the work to provide written responses. They can be thought of as focused journaling, the writing down of specific thoughts and/or meditations relating to their personal plan of recovery or therapy in the context of God's word.

For 12 step program sponsors, although these exercises have a suggested step that the author believes might be appropriate, the sponsor can choose to use them as he or she sees fit. As such they help the sponsor to encourage their program participant look at a wide range of recovery topics more closely. We therefore suggest that the sponsee owns a personal copy of this book and the sponsor assigns exercises as appropriate, giving the sponsee time to complete one and coming back together to discuss the results and see what God may be revealing.

For Program or Plan Participants

These exercises are designed to assist and guide a personal introspection into an individual's heart, mind and will. This is always best done under the guidance of the Holy Spirit. This is why we suggest that before a person begins an exercise, they say a short prayer asking God through His Spirit to reveal what needs to be known or looked at in going through the work involved.

There is no right or wrong about any of the answers. The best results for a person doing this exercise come when they are open and honest with God, themselves and their program guide and give themselves time to do the work. Our experience suggests a minimum of a week per exercise.

General Instructions to Book Users

This is a workbook of sorts. While we have put in space for users to write in the book, the intent is for those doing the exercises to write their responses in other locations. Examples of this might be personal journals or recovery folders; something personal and private to an individual.

We do suggest that those assigning exercises might write in the book of a program participant or other end user. Sometimes encouraging words can be added; or extra commentary on the scriptures being used or possibly more individualized direction and instructions. Each exercise has space allocated for this purpose.

Being thorough in doing the work, as in all work, yields the most optimal results for an individual using these exercises. Use the book with a view to being healed from something or overcoming a serious struggle. This is the kind of thing that the Apostle Paul was talking about in Philippians 2:12-13. As we adopt this attitude of working with an expectation of the Spirit doing something in us, the work becomes a part of our personal sanctification; God's saving work that He performs with us and in us throughout our lives.

You may notice that some of the exercises may be similar to one another; this is by design. Our experience in recovery work suggests that looking at the same problem from different perspectives is advantageous in achieving good program results. Included in each exercise is a short list of emotion and attitude words that could be used in an individual's written exercise response. At the back of the book, Addendum 3 contains a good selection of emotion/attitude words for reference.

Finally, we suggest that an individual keep all notes, answers and responses separate and private from other personal documentation as these exercises will reveal things to you that others may not understand and therefore misinterpret.

This page intentionally left blank.

Exercise 1

2 Samuel 9:2

<u>Ziba – Untrustworthy Servant</u>

2 Sam 9:2 - Now there was a servant of the house of Saul whose name was Ziba, and they called him to David; and the king said to him, "Are you Ziba?" And he said, "I am your servant." NASU

<u>Guiding Commentary</u> – Ziba is one of those side characters in a story that changes outcomes of situations through ungodly behaviors and negatively impacts those around him, even putting them at risk.

Ziba appears just as David takes over as king. He was a servant of Saul, the previous king, who had tried to kill David. The practice in the Middle East back then was for the triumphant king to kill the entire family of the vanquished king, which included the servants and their families, so they couldn't reclaim the throne. In our verse, Ziba, who was probably very nervous, quickly says that he is David's servant. As the story goes on (read 2 Sam 9:1-13, 2 Sam 16:1-4) we see that Ziba somehow acquired the previous king's possessions, but David took them back and gave them to Saul's crippled son, Mephibosheth, and put Ziba in charge of the household. Then through a series of circumstances, Ziba had another opportunity to lie (2 Sam 16) to David and ended up with Saul's possessions again, and put Mephibosheth at risk of being executed.

Ziba was a liar, cheater (betrayer) and thief who fooled even the brightest people around him. He was an opportunist who built a family fortune on ungodly behavior, and his entire household, consisting of at least 15 sons and 20 servants, probably about 100 people in all, went along with all the deception for their own personal gain. Scripture doesn't tell us that he came to a bad end, this is no fairy story, this is reality, and sometimes bad behavior leads to worldly success.

<u>The Exercise</u> – Are you a Ziba, or have you been a Ziba? If you are in recovery the answer has to be yes. In this exercise we are going to look at three simple questions:

- What have you stolen?

- How have you lied?
- Who have you betrayed?

Write out the answers to these questions, detailing out as much of this as your spiritual guide suggests. We recommend you limit yourself to two lengthy paragraphs for each question.

Finally, write out a prayer to God that asks Him to reveal any remaining desire to lie, cheat and steal that you may have, and pray it each day for a week. Whatever God reveals to you ought to then be journaled and discussed with a sponsor, mentor or counselor.

Sponsor Notes: _____

_____

_____

Useful Feeling Words:

- Guilt, Shame, Unworthy, Afraid, Reluctant

Useful Attitudinal Words:

- Forgiveness, Worthlessness, Anxious, Embarrassed, Nervous

My Pre-exercise Notes: _____

_____

_____

_____

_____

The suggested step for Exercise 1 is Step 4.

Exercise 2

2 Samuel 6:14, 16 and 20

<u>Michal - Condemning Wife</u>

2 Sam 6:14, 16, 20 - And David danced before the Lord with all his might. And David was wearing a linen ephod. 16 As the ark of the Lord came into the city of David, Michal the daughter of Saul looked out of the window and saw King David leaping and dancing before the Lord, and she despised him in her heart. 20 And David returned to bless his household. But Michal the daughter of Saul came out to meet David and said, "How the king of Israel honored himself today, uncovering himself today before the eyes of his servants' female servants, as one of the vulgar fellows shamelessly uncovers himself!" ESV

<u>Guiding Commentary</u> – Michal was David's first wife. She was the daughter of Israel's first king and her marriage to the future king, David, was much like a modern era arranged marriage where the girl marries the heir apparent to keep the family business together. Unfortunately she had a critical spirit, meaning she carried a condemning attitude around with her.

In the example we are looking at here, David has taken most of his clothes off, and is dancing with joy before God and the people because a great spiritual event was taking place. The Ark of the Covenant was coming to town to be permanently housed in a future temple. God's presence was pictured as being located in the middle of the Ark on the mercy seat, and so this was a great honor for Jerusalem.

Michal missed the point of the event and only saw a mostly naked David; she despised him for this, and followed it up with a condemning statement, calling her husband, the king, shameless and vulgar in a public forum. She most likely was feeling deeply embarrassed about the fact that her husband was involved in this brazen act of near nudity.

In this she was placing herself in God's place, for God saw this and said nothing to David, implying that He accepted David's worship. If this were to happen today, we would say she was trying to be the Holy Spirit in David's life.

<u>The Exercise</u> – Write about how you used to be like Michal, and about how you deal with your own condemning spirit today. Give some actual examples from your life. Speak with some people that you trust, and that know you, to get some objective input.

Now read Romans 8:1 and write a paragraph on how you compare to what God says about Himself on this issue. Then read 2 Cor 10:5 and write about what you do, and what this verse says to do with your condemning thoughts. Finally, write a promise before God about any changes you would like to make about condemnation of others in your own life.

Sponsor Notes: _____

_____

_____

Useful Feeling Words:

- Condemned, Put-down, Shame, Worthless, Guilty

Useful Attitudinal Words:

- Judgmentalism, Pride, Hopefulness, Embarrassment, Free

My Pre-exercise Notes: _____

_____

_____

_____

_____

The suggested step for Exercise 2 is Step 6.

Exercise 3

Jonah 1:1-3(a)

<u>Jonah – Disobedient Grump</u>

Jonah 1:1-3(a) - Now the word of the Lord came to Jonah the son of Amittai, saying, "Arise, go to Nineveh, that great city, and call out against it, for their evil has come up before me." But Jonah rose to flee to Tarshish from the presence of the Lord. ESV

<u>Guiding Commentary</u> – Jonah was a grumpy prophet. He was an Israelite, and God called him to preach the gospel to Nineveh. Now at that time Nineveh was the center of the Assyrian empire, the Assyrians (Ninevites) were Israel's chief nemesis. (FYI Nineveh is located in modern Iraq, near Mosul.) The Ninevites were cruel, sadistic and thoroughly immoral; and poor Jonah was told by God to travel several hundred miles to preach repentance to his enemy and they would be saved.

Jonah basically told God, "there is no way I'm going there, and there is no way I want to have a part in saving them", and so he disobeyed and took off, literally. He headed out of town on a ship, and we probably all know what happened. There was a storm, the ship was at risk of sinking, and eventually Jonah admitted it was his doing. (Jonah 1:4-16) So he volunteered to be thrown overboard, and that is when he was swallowed by a great fish (v17). Eventually Jonah obeyed, although he really didn't want to, and all of Nineveh was saved.

Isn't that so like us in recovery? When we know that God has told us to do something, we respond by going a different direction, some of us even try to flee from God. God speaks to us in recovery through four main ways; the people in our recovery fellowship, the program itself, the word of God and His Holy Spirit. Often He will speak in more than one way, and more than one time. Being a Jonah doesn't get us anywhere but stuck in our own version of the belly of a great fish. We ought to trust God by being obedient, because He can see our future, and we can't. We ought to apologize to Him for all the habitual disobedience we have indulged in over the years.

<u>The Exercise</u> – Our first task here is to admit our habitual disobedience to God and His instructions. Write a letter to God, confessing your historical disobedience and any area you are struggling in today. Be specific, but don't write more than two pages.

Take this letter into a time of prayer and meditation, starting with 15 minutes of silence, then read it to him aloud, and offer your apologies. Conclude this time with another 15 minutes of silence waiting to see how the Holy Spirit responds. Treat this whole time as if you were making amends to God face to face.

Discuss this exercise with your mentor or other spiritual adviser.

Sponsor Notes: _____

_____

_____

Useful Feeling Words:

- Anxious, Fear, Stressed, Rebellious, Resentful

Useful Attitudinal Words:

- Disobedience, Stubborn, Resentfulness, Arrogance, Apathetic

My Pre-exercise Notes: _____

_____

_____

_____

_____

The suggested step for Exercise 3 is Step 9.

Exercise 4

2 Samuel 11:8-9

<u>Uriah – Dead People-Pleaser</u>

2 Sam 11:8-9 - Then David said to Uriah, "Go down to your house and wash your feet." And Uriah went out of the king's house, and there followed him a present from the king. But Uriah slept at the door of the king's house with all the servants of his lord, and did not go down to his house. ESV

<u>Guiding Commentary</u> – Uriah is one of those sad characters in scripture. He was faithful to his king, his employer, so much so that ultimately it was a major factor in his early and avoidable death. King David, in order to cover up his sin of sleeping with Bathsheba, Uriah's wife, and the consequent pregnancy, arranged for Uriah to come back from the war for a conjugal visit. Uriah, not knowing any of what had happened didn't head back to his wife, but instead slept in the palace's servant's quarters as a mark of his dedication to David.

This caused a problem for David, because Bathsheba was pregnant by him. Eventually David chose to get Uriah killed in battle and take Bathsheba for himself. Read the whole thing in 2 Sam 11:1-27, it is like something from a modern day soap opera.

In recovery, both secular and Christian, we see our Uriah's. People who exhibit codependency in the form of dedication to others to the point of not taking care of their own family, allowing others to use them and even harming themselves. This is an extraordinarily hard habit to break, mostly because it is a deeply ingrained issue, and because it often looks socially acceptable.

<u>The Exercise</u> – In this exercise we are going to inventory our people-pleasing activities. First, go back to pre-recovery times and list some examples, up to ten, of the people pleasing you engaged in. Give your behavior a name, for example "approval seeking from employer", write a description of it and lastly identify the people that were hurt because of it.

Here are some example words that may be useful in describing what you were looking for while engaging in people-pleasing; acceptance, affirmation; affection, admiration; comfort, respect and support.

Next do the same for the time you have been in recovery.

Finally, write about any patterns you see in these examples and discuss them with your sponsor, mentor or counselor.

Sponsor Notes: _____

_____

_____

Useful Feeling Words:

- Affirmed, Accepted, Rejected, Comforted, Supported

Useful Attitudinal Words:

- Angry, Ashamed, Resentfulness, Rebelliousness, Pride

My Pre-exercise Notes: _____

_____

_____

_____

_____

The suggested step for Exercise 4 is Step 4.

Exercise 5

Matthew 14:29-31

<u>Peter – Doubting Rock</u>

Matt 14:29-31 - He said, "Come." So Peter got out of the boat and walked on the water and came to Jesus. But when he saw the wind, he was afraid, and beginning to sink he cried out, "Lord, save me." Jesus immediately reached out his hand and took hold of him, saying to him, "O you of little faith, why did you doubt?" ESV

<u>Guiding Commentary</u> – Peter, which is from the Greek name Petros, meaning rock, was an impetuous fellow. In multiple places in the Gospels he is recorded to have leapt into action, and then dealt with the consequences later. Isn't that so like many of us in recovery? In this scene, he gets out of a boat and while focusing on Jesus, walks on water. Then he has that moment that all impulsives have when they realize what they have got themselves into. He takes his focus away from Jesus and begins to sink. This is when we see that famous phrase, "O you of little faith, why did you doubt?"

I have no doubt that if Peter lived in our century he would be an addict. He has so many of the behavioral characteristics of an impulsive and immature adult, the kind that often ends up in serious compulsive activities.

Peter, at this point in the New Testament story, is an example of a person that is controlled by his emotions. Just like so many of us, he did what he felt like doing, without thinking things through or counting the cost. After Christ rose from the dead Peter became a different man, he became a man controlled by the Spirit, piloted by faith and focused on Jesus.

<u>The Exercise</u> – To start this exercise we are going to ask you to write down up to two paragraphs of your personal speculation about what emotions Peter may have been feeling during this whole encounter with Jesus. Which emotion would you guess was in charge of his actions as he jumped out of the boat, which one was in charge as he sank and what might he have felt when he was rescued?

Now, go back to the time when you were acting out and guess at the kind of feelings you were dealing with before you acted out, during the acting out and after it was over. Give at least two separate examples.

Finally, when you are tempted to act out now, what do you feel? Write a paragraph or two on this, telling your spiritual guide what feelings you have, what you do with them and how the Holy Spirit is involved in helping you.

Sponsor Notes: _____

_____

_____

Useful Feeling Words:

- Impulsive, Reckless, Tempted, Immature, Hopeless

Useful Attitudinal Words:

- Rebelliousness, Impetuosity, Risk-taker, Compulsiveness, Angry

My Pre-exercise Notes: _____

_____

_____

_____

The suggested step for Exercise 5 is Step 6.

Exercise 6

Esther 4:15-16

<u>Esther- Fasting Queen</u>

Est 4:15-16 - Then Esther told them to reply to Mordecai, "Go, gather all the Jews to be found in Susa, and hold a fast on my behalf, and do not eat or drink for three days, night or day. I and my young women will also fast as you do. Then I will go to the king, though it is against the law, and if I perish, I perish." ESV

<u>Guiding Commentary</u> – Esther (also known as Hadassah) was one of the Jewish exiles living in the capital of the ancient Persian empire, Susa (modern day Shush). Through circumstance, which the scriptures suggest was organized by God, she became the wife of Ahaseurus, better known by us as Xerxes, who was the king. The prime minister of Persia, Haman, had craftily put Xerxes in a political corner and was about to get all the Jews rounded up and exterminated. And this is when these famous lines are uttered by Mordecai, Esther's uncle; Est 4:14 - And who knows whether you have not come to the kingdom for such a time as this?" ESV

In the story Esther is faced with having to break the law, putting her life in danger, by speaking up about the injustice which is about to happen. Esther calls for a three day fast, where all Jews were asked to go without food and drink for three days and nights, as spiritual preparation for her having to face this challenge.

Fasting is a big challenge for us in Christian recovery, because it involves temporarily giving up something that we need or want, and that is not easy for us. Yet scripture is clear in calling all believers to fast and pray with the purpose of connecting with God for spiritual reasons. We in Christian recovery have many occasions, many spiritual events, which would probably be put in a clearer perspective if we fasted ahead of time, for example, before we begin a moral inventory, before we confess our shortcomings or before we give amends.

<u>The Exercise</u> – Choose a moment in your recovery to go through a three day fast, in this exercise we are suggesting to do this after you have finished your moral inventory and before confession of shortcomings. If you have any limiting medical condition, consult with your physician first. Work with your sponsor, mentor or other spiritual adviser to select dates to do this, to plan what you are going to fast

from, and what your purpose for fasting might be. Pray with at least two friends from your recovery fellowship ahead of this for accountability purposes.

As you go through the fast, journal what you think the Holy Spirit might be saying to you. This journaling ought to begin before you start, and continue up to the moment you break the fast at the planned time. After all this, record your fasting experience for your future reference, and discuss this fasting exercise with your spiritual adviser.

Sponsor Notes: _____

_____

_____

Useful Feeling Words:

- Afraid, Apprehensive, Inquisitive, Interested, Thoughtful

Useful Attitudinal Words:

- Disobedience, Anxiety, Excited, Expectant, Joyful

My Pre-exercise Notes: _____

_____

_____

_____

_____

The suggested step for Exercise 6 is Step 5.

Exercise 7

Genesis 15:5-6

<u>Abram – Friend of God</u>

Gen 15:5-6 - And he brought him outside and said, "Look toward heaven, and number the stars, if you are able to number them." Then he said to him, "So shall your offspring be." And he believed the Lord, and he counted it to him as righteousness. ESV

<u>Guiding Commentary</u> – Abram, later called Abraham, was called righteous by God because he believed God's promise. God kept His promise to Abram, in that he became the single point ancestor of the Ishmaelites (forerunner to the Arabs of today) and the Israelites (Hebrews or Jews). Later in scripture we see that Abraham was called by God "friend." (James 2:23), the only person directly called that. The blessings; of the two great nations, material wealth and the personal friendship with God Almighty came to Abraham because he believed God.

In Christian recovery we are asked to believe God. Not believe in God, for even the demons believe in God, however at one point in time, they didn't believe God, they believed a lie. To believe God is to have faith that what He says He will do will happen. It is having a 100% certainty that His promises to us will come to pass.

Do you believe God, or are you reserving some parts of your life for yourself, so that you can control them? Do you know that when any of us does that we shut Him out of being able to bless us in ways we can't imagine? It seems from scripture that God works this way because He wants us to be able to say that we chose Him and not that we are His puppets, which are things that He created and made to follow Him.

<u>The Exercise</u> – Take a look back in your life start with as far back as you can remember and write out a faith progression. This is simply a series of statements that describe your faith (defined as your level of belief in God) and how it has changed over time. It may even have gone up then down then back up.

Now write about how your level of faith impacts your willingness to do things God's way, to believe Him and His promises. Be as openly honest as you can, starting with the understanding that God knows the truth anyway. Look at Luke 18:9-14 for inspiration.

Finally, answer the question, do I really want to be a friend of Almighty God? Assuming you say yes, write out a prayer asking for God to help you with your unbelief, so that you might be able to not only say you are His friend but you will carry a deep and unshakeable conviction that you are. Share this whole exercise with a couple of godly friends, then talk with your spiritual adviser.

Sponsor Notes: _____

_____

_____

Useful Feeling Words:

- Guilty, Fearful, Unbelieving, Stressed, Hopeful

Useful Attitudinal Words:

- Thankful, Fearful, Passive, Reluctant, Hopefulness

My Pre-exercise Notes: _____

_____

_____

_____

_____

The suggested step for Exercise 7 is Step 3.

Exercise 8

John 18:33-35

<u>Pilate – Judgmental Blamer</u>

John 18:33-35 - So Pilate entered his headquarters again and called Jesus and said to him, "Are you the King of the Jews?" Jesus answered, "Do you say this of your own accord, or did others say it to you about me?" Pilate answered, "Am I a Jew? Your own nation and the chief priests have delivered you over to me. What have you done?" ESV

<u>Guiding Commentary</u> – Pilate, better known as Pontius Pilate, was the governor of the province of Judea and was known for being a cruel and unjust administrator. For him, the assignment of ruling Judea was an expression of Caesar's disapproval and disfavor, which came out as resentment toward the Jews. Pilate is a central figure in the story of Jesus' last week, and for this reason he is found in all four gospels. It is he that authorized the legal execution of Jesus.

Pilate is the historical figure that said to Jesus, "What is truth?" when he was standing, in spiritual blindness, next to the God/man who was truth incarnate. (Jn 18:38) He is also the man that washed his hands and declared that he was innocent of spilling Jesus' blood. (Mt 27:24) In our focus verses Pilate made a very human assumption, that just because Jesus was in front of him, delivered by the Jewish leaders, that He was to blame for something.

In the story of Jesus' last day we see the Jewish spiritual leaders blaming Jesus, King Herod, blaming those leaders and the Roman authorities blaming the Jews and Jesus. Lots of blaming, but no taking of responsibility! In Christian recovery one of the major lessons we must learn is that of being responsible for our actions. As an fyi, the responsibility rule is; "We are responsible for ourselves and to others."

<u>The Exercise</u> – Take a look back to when you were in the depths of acting out and make a list of things that you were responsible for but didn't do well with (up to ten items). For each item on the list identify who you believed was responsible for your misfortune or behaviors at that time. For example you may have been blaming a spouse or parents or boss.

Next, discuss, by writing out your current personal evaluation, as to whether you still blame others for your actions. Include feeling or attitude words that might be recognizable to you as you do this. (For example, I'm bitter toward my parents because they drank in front of me.)

Next, write out a statement of repentance for blaming others, and a declaration of your intent to stop blaming others for things that are your responsibility to take care of. Pray this for yourself in your own way, once a day for a week.

Sponsor Notes: _____

_____

_____

Useful Feeling Words:

- Troubled, Sincere, Repentant, Grateful, Condemned

Useful Attitudinal Words:

- Anxious, Rebelliousness, Unforgiveness, Joyless, Innocent

My Pre-exercise Notes: _____

_____

_____

_____

_____

The suggested step for Exercise 8 is Step 4.

Exercise 9

John 1:46-49

<u>Nathanael – Honest Seeker</u>

John 1:46-49 - Nathanael said to him, "Can anything good come out of Nazareth?" Philip said to him, "Come and see." Jesus saw Nathanael coming toward him and said of him, "Behold, an Israelite indeed, in whom there is no deceit!" Nathanael said to him, "How do you know me?" Jesus answered him, "Before Philip called you, when you were under the fig tree, I saw you." Nathanael answered him, "Rabbi, you are the Son of God! You are the King of Israel!" ESV

<u>Guiding Commentary</u> – Nathanael, possibly better written as Nathan'El, "God has given", has a unique place in scripture. He first makes a seemingly derogatory remark about Jesus' hometown of Nazareth, and Jesus replies "Look at this guy, he is an honest man." Nathanael responds by asking a great question, "How do you know me?" Notice here that Nathanael implicitly acknowledges that he is an honest man, always seeking truth, and that he knew that Jesus recognized that characteristic even before they had established a relationship. Jesus tells Nathanael that He saw Nathanael in his personal quiet time under a fig tree. That prompted Nathanael to immediately follow Jesus, because He was truth personified.

One of the great truths of life is found right here. This is a truth that many struggle to understand and worse, agree with. For those of us in Christian recovery it is vital that we get this if we want to be healed.

When we live a life of deceit, we live a life of lie after lie, we become liars! Read that carefully again. We start by lying, which is a behavior, as we continue to behave with deceit, we eventually become liars. We go from <u>exhibiting</u> a bad behavior to <u>being</u> that behavior. When we get to that psychological place, our natural state is that we <u>are</u> liars and this has consequences. When we are liars, we have trouble speaking truth in any situation, we have trouble recognizing truth in others, we often don't believe God and we cannot heal. This is why we say for all those in recovery, "Honesty before sobriety." (Also see Jn 8:44-45)

<u>The Exercise</u> – Do you agree with the principle that those who lie eventually become liars? Answer that in writing through your own experiences. Start with how you lied before recovery, detailing out specific examples of your lying and its consequences. Show how your inner person got corrupted by your own lies, and possibly the lies of others. Discuss your emotional response to thinking about yourself as <u>being</u> a liar. If you've been in recovery for a while, write about you level of lying compared to pre-recovery days. Finally write two paragraphs, the first begins with this phrase; "I am honest because." The second begins "I am still dishonest in." Discuss thoroughly with your sponsor or other adviser.

Sponsor Notes: _____

_____

_____

Useful Feeling Words:

- Powerless, Hopeless, Guilty, Ashamed, Unworthy

Useful Attitudinal Words:

- Deceitfulness, Valueless, Depressed, Resentfulness, Pride

My Pre-exercise Notes: _____

_____

_____

_____

_____

The suggested step for Exercise 9 is Step 1.

Exercise 10

1 Samuel 17:4

<u>Goliath – Invincible Corpse</u>

1 Sam 17:4 - And there came out from the camp of the Philistines a champion named Goliath of Gath, whose height was six cubits and a span.   ESV

<u>Guiding Commentary</u> – Goliath was a true physical giant, his strength was such that the tip of his spear was six hundred shekels, about eighteen pounds twelve ounces. He was probably between nine feet six and eleven feet, depending on how one measures a cubit. Although he lived with the ancient enemy of Israel, the Philistines, he was most likely from the tribe of giants called Anaks. In this scripture (read 1 Sam 17:4-58 for the full story) Goliath came out and taunted the Israelites as he was to do for 40 continuous days. It was common practice for enemies to send their champion into a one-on-one fight with the victor's side winning the war. This avoided the very dangerous reality that both sides could get wiped out, making them easy targets for a third enemy.

We all know the story, the young boy, David, goes out and kills the giant Goliath under God's protection, and the Israelites win the war. This story, while it is an actual historical event, is also symbolic for humanity, if they care to listen. It is one person, plus God, defeating something that cannot be overcome any other way.

This is a great figurative story for us in recovery. The giant is something big that we have to fight and that we know we cannot defeat with our own resources and power. If we have anything in our lives that determines how our day goes, where we spend our time or money or how we think, feel and choose, then we have a giant. God could be our giant, but we all know that if He were, we would never have got into recovery in the first place. No, our giants are the compulsions or addictions that we struggle with; they could also be our challenges trusting or being intimate with a spouse after a betrayal. Whatever they are, they can only be defeated with God's help.

<u>The Exercise</u> – Write about the giants in your life, only consider up to three giants, one-by-one. Using feeling words when possible, talk about when you first remember the giants appearing, when you started to have a sense they were

stalking you or taunting you. Write about the times when you took on your giants and failed to defeat them, how did you feel afterwards? Write about when you figured out that you couldn't defeat them by yourself, and what you did about that. Next write about how you are dealing with your giants today.

Finally write out a prayer for yourself asking for God to help you fight your giants. Be specific, name your giants and state what you want God to do for you. Pray this for yourself for a week, and also ask three people you trust to pray it for you too. Discuss the results of this exercise with your sponsor or other spiritual guide.

Sponsor Notes: _____

_____

_____

Useful Feeling Words:

- Impotent, Willing, Desperate, Fearful, Angry

Useful Attitudinal Words:

- Vulnerable, Nervous, Powerlessness, Weak, Disbelieving

My Pre-exercise Notes: _____

_____

_____

_____

The suggested step for Exercise 10 is Step 2.

Exercise 11

Luke 19:8-9

<u>Zacchaeus – Repentant Taxman</u>

Luke 19:8-9 - And Zacchaeus stood and said to the Lord, "Behold, Lord, the half of my goods I give to the poor. And if I have defrauded anyone of anything, I restore it fourfold." ESV

<u>Guiding Commentary</u> – Zacchaeus was a short man with a big bank account. Most of this came from his tax collecting activities where he was the conduit between the regular tax collectors and the governing authorities, and he skimmed off the top, or took a personal commission. This meant that he was a thief, a thief with a high legal position. In the story (Lk 19:1-10) we see some important truths.

First, Zacchaeus was very keen to see Jesus; he had to climb up a tree. To put that in perspective, it would be like a high level IRS agent, a high paid bureaucrat, used to getting his way, having to demean himself. Second, Jesus saw him up the tree, and recognized that Zacchaeus was ready to repent. Third, when all the regular folk saw that Jesus was going to the home of Zacchaeus they condemned Him. Fourth, Zacchaeus, as a result of his encounter with Jesus, was able to shift from a desire to repent to a choice to make amends.

The fifth and last point has a large significance for us in Christian recovery. As a result of this choice to make amends Jesus indicates that salvation came to the entire household of Zacchaeus. While Jesus was undoubtedly stating the household of Zacchaeus was saved, as in born again, our application is different. For a Christ follower who takes the path of repentance and making amends the salvation is in the form of sanctification, or a cleaning up of our internal darker places.

<u>The Exercise</u> – As you come to the point in your recovery program where it is time to go say sorry, to ask how much you hurt someone and request forgiveness, which is called making amends, what feelings come up? Write about your fears, anxieties or apprehensions about doing this. Discuss your internal willingness to go forward into meetings with people you may have damaged. Are you worried about rejection, anger, hatefulness or unforgiveness from the people on your amends list?

Include any thoughts you may have on how you expect things will go when you start making amends. (If you've already begun making amends or completed them, try to do this exercise by thinking back to before you started.)

Next write about your expectations of what God might do in you or those you make amends to, particularly bearing in mind what happened in Zacchaeus' life when he became willing. Does his story inspire or encourage you?

Finally, write out a personal prayer for yourself about having the courage and willingness to go make amends to those on your list. Pray it for yourself each day for a week.

Sponsor Notes: _____

_____

_____

Useful Feeling Words:

- Weak, Scared, Excited, Apprehensive, Cautious

Useful Attitudinal Words:

- Cautiousness, Fearful, Joyful, Tentativeness, Courageous

My Pre-exercise Notes: _____

_____

_____

_____

_____

The suggested step for Exercise 11 is Step 8.

Exercise 12

2 Timothy 1:5-7

<u>Timothy – Faithful Child</u>

2 Tim 1:5-7 - I am reminded of your sincere faith, a faith that dwelt first in your grandmother Lois and your mother Eunice and now, I am sure, dwells in you as well. For this reason I remind you to fan into flame the gift of God, which is in you through the laying on of my hands, for God gave us a spirit not of fear but of power and love and self-control. ESV

<u>Guiding Commentary</u> – Timothy was most likely the Apostle Paul's favorite "child in the faith", a younger man whom he mentored. Paul spent about 3 years with him in Ephesus, which was at the time the gateway into Asia, and a very spiritually active city, but not in a good way. Paul calls Timothy's faith "sincere" a description of Timothy's motivations. Timothy approached his faith like a child; read Jesus' words in Luke 18:17 – "Truly, I say to you, whoever does not receive the kingdom of God like a child shall not enter it." ESV

In our scripture we see Paul connecting faith and how active the Holy Spirit is able to be in us. While it is true that God can do anything He wants, it is also a practical spiritual reality that we can get in God's way in our own lives (1 Thess 5:19). Here Paul says to fan into flame the gift of God, He is speaking about the Holy Spirit who is pictured sometimes as a fire that inflames our passions for God. He then tells that that the Holy Spirit imparts to us, not fear, but power, love and self-control. (See also Gal 5:22-23)

The take away from this is that in our Christian recovery, we are to adopt a childlike faith. Having an attitude that we are children, that God is our Father, and that He is going to help remove our fears, gives us the power to overcome our struggles, feed us His unconditional love and helps us to remain sober.

<u>The Exercise</u> – Write about your faith, using these questions as a guide. Did you have a childlike faith before recovery, or were you a doubter, a skeptic, a cynic or simply ignorant of what God says? Now that you are in recovery, are you willing to be childlike, are you willing to really believe that what God says in His word is true and it is going to help you? Have you reached the point where you realize that

you are a barrier to your own healing, and that you have to put all your old way aside and do life the way God says, like an obedient child? Discuss all these things, be brave and be honest like a child. Bring in other relevant scriptures if you can think of some.

Now write about what you believe the power of the Holy Spirit will mean to you in your recovery, write about what God's unconditional love will look like in your life of recovery, and write about what self-control means to you. Finally write out a prayer asking God to help you become childlike in your faith and in your recovery program. Pray it for yourself for a week.

Sponsor Notes: _____

_____

_____

Useful Feeling Words:

- Favored, Childlike, Peaceful, Intimate, Appreciative

Useful Attitudinal Words:

- Reverent, Believing, Optimistic, Impassioned, Free

My Pre-exercise Notes: _____

_____

_____

_____

_____

The suggested step for Exercise 12 is Step 2.

Exercise 13

Judges 3:11-12

Othniel – Godly Protector

Judg 3:11-12 - So the land had rest forty years. Then Othniel the son of Kenaz died. And the people of Israel again did what was evil in the sight of the Lord, and the Lord strengthened Eglon the king of Moab against Israel, because they had done what was evil in the sight of the Lord. ESV

Guiding Commentary – If we don't include Joshua, then Othniel is the first "judge" of Israel after the conquest of Canaan. Judges were "hero-leaders" raised up for God's purposes in moving God's people from their apostate ways back into fellowship with Him. (Judg 2:16) Othniel was the son of Caleb's brother, Kenaz, and therefore was most likely to be one of the individuals that crossed the Jordan into the Promised Land and was part of the conquest of Canaan.

In our story (Judg 3:7-14) Othniel is lifted up by God to lead Israel from their apostasy, or backsliding, defeat the enemies and restore theocracy. As a result Israel had peace and prosperity for the next 40 years. Then Othniel died, and the people slid right back into idol worship and other evil activities. So God disciplined them by strengthening the king of Moab (part of modern day Jordan) who, along with the Ammonites and Amalekites, defeated them and put them into a form of servitude.

There is a picture here of how it goes for some of us in Christian recovery. We move out of slavery, our Egypt, and into the wilderness, our early recovery, then into the Promised Land, where we have overcome our major compulsions. We get relief from our issues, we feel that life is better, and we start to let our guard down. Sometimes our old compulsions rear their ugly head, and sometimes we develop new compulsions, and we start to let go of God, we backslide into some form of personal slavery. God, who never lets us go, brings discipline into our life, sometimes through the hurtful events of life or the painful intervention of others. We have to recognize our faults and our backsliding, repent and confess, and restart recovery.

The Exercise – Pray for God's help doing this exercise for 24 hours, then reflect on your recovery and perform a self-assessment of how well you have stayed away from behaviors that hurt; include any accountability partners and your sponsor for input if you wish. Write down, in brutal honesty, all that you discover about how your recovery has gone. Here are some useful questions: Have you had trouble remaining sober, do you experience euphoric recall, are you easily triggered, are your thoughts pure, and are you engaging in new compulsions? Include details of any slips or relapses that you experienced, and any sense that God is disciplining you, and if He is, how He is doing it.

Discuss this with your sponsor or mentor before during and after going through this.

Sponsor Notes: _____

_____

_____

Useful Feeling Words:

- Tempted, Anxious, Triggered, Disappointed, Disillusioned

Useful Attitudinal Words:

- Weak-hearted, Desperateness, Pessimistic, Compulsiveness, Embarassment

My Pre-exercise Notes: _____

_____

_____

_____

The suggested step for Exercise 13 is Step 10.

Exercise 14

Acts 5:33-34

<u>Gamaliel – Secret Agent</u>

Acts 5:33-34 - When they heard this, they were enraged and wanted to kill them. But a Pharisee in the council named Gamaliel, a teacher of the law held in honor by all the people, stood up and gave orders to put the men outside for a little while. ESV

<u>Guiding Commentary</u> – Gamaliel, called here a teacher of the law held in high honor by all the people, was probably the most prominent theologian of his day. He was the man who taught the Apostle Paul (before Paul's conversion to Christianity); this is revealed by Paul in Acts 22:3 who basically credits Gamaliel with stoking the fire for God in him during his time of learning. In this Gamaliel was God's secret agent, so secret that he didn't know he was educating the person destined to be the world's greatest missionary and writer of over half of the New Testament. Gamaliel most likely was part of the ruling council when Jesus was unjustly condemned to death, although there is no evidence that he was part of the plot, but he certainly would know what was going on with the disciples and their preaching.

In our focus passage we see Gamaliel stepping in and protecting the disciples after they had just truthfully accused the council of murdering Jesus. (Read the whole passage in Acts 5:27-42) Gamaliel rightly and wisely says; let them be, if this movement is not of God it will fail, if it is of God we would be fighting God. Again, Gamaliel is doing God's secret work, but unknowingly.

Sometimes we don't appreciate the reality that God can use us in secret in our recovery situations. We know that we can be thought of as Christ's ambassadors (2 Cor 5:20), but we rarely understand that God may use us or our story in another person's life in secret ways. We are therefore his overt agents and his covert agents. As we attend our meetings and interact with others in our lives let us be mindful that our God delights in using His people in ways that only He can make happen.

The Exercise – Write about times in your recovery that you have been influenced and helped by others. Split this exercise between when you openly knew someone was overtly helping you, as an ambassador might, when you were helped with the knowledge of the other person. Provide some detailed examples for your sponsor.

Next write about how you have tried to help others during your recovery. Again segment the writing between times you have openly helped other, times you have quietly behind the scenes tried to help and times when you realized you may have unconsciously helped another person. Include expressions of feelings you had or now have about helping others and God using you and your story for His purposes.

Sponsor Notes: _____

_____

_____

Useful Feeling Words:

- Grateful, Thankful, Accepted, Shame, Insecure

Useful Attitudinal Words:

- Gratefulness, Secure, Optimistic, Solemn, Disdainfulness

My Pre-exercise Notes: _____

_____

_____

_____

_____

The suggested step for Exercise 14 is Step 12.

Exercise 15

Genesis 4:6-7

<u>Cain – First Murderer</u>

Gen 4:6-7 - The Lord said to Cain, "Why are you angry, and why has your face fallen? If you do well, will you not be accepted? And if you do not do well, sin is crouching at the door. Its desire is for you, but you must rule over it." ESV

<u>Guiding Commentary</u> – The sad story of Cain has a significant impact for us in Christian recovery, if we allow it. Cain was the first man ever born, he was the first son for Adam and Eve and he was the first murderer, when he killed his little brother Abel. What we may not see in the story of Cain is that he was the first person recorded to have what gamblers call a "tell."

A "tell" is a behavior that a person can be relied on to consistently do in certain stressful circumstances. In poker it is an unconscious action that is thought to betray an attempted deception. In our language a tell is a lie.

Cain's tell is found in Gen 4:5 – "Cain was very angry, and his face fell." (ESV) He got angry and he exhibited a fallen or downcast expression. Right after this he tricked Abel into going with him to the fields, and murdered him.

One of the great deceptions or denials that an addict lives in is that they really believe that others cannot see when they are lying. For all of us in recovery, Christian or not, we need to come to terms with the truth that we have tells. We are using the plural here because it is likely that we have more than one.

<u>The Exercise</u> – In this exercise we are going to look at trying to figure out our tell or tells. Before you go any further with this, read Proverbs 27:6.

Go to the people who know you the best, that you trust and care enough about you to speak truth into your life. Try to get at least three people on your list, and if you are married, include your spouse. Ask them this question. (You may have to insist that they answer this truthfully and deeply, as sometimes friends don't want to hurt, so you may have to show them Pr 27:6)

- What behavior have you noticed I seem to engage in right before I lie to you or about something?

Write down a synopsis of your discussion with each of them and your response to the whole exercise. Were you surprised to discover that those that love or care for you do so even though they know when you are lying? Finally, discuss this with you spiritual advisor.

Sponsor Notes: _____

_____

_____

Useful Feeling Words:

- Prideful, Ashamed, Powerless, Vulnerable, Uncontrolled

Useful Attitudinal Words:

- Pride, Selfishness, Hopelessness, Hard-Hearted, Pessimistic

My Pre-exercise Notes: _____

_____

_____

_____

The suggested step for Exercise 15 is Step 1.

Exercise 16

1 Kings 16:29-30

Ahab – Inherited Evil

1 Kings 16:29-30 - In the thirty-eighth year of Asa king of Judah, Ahab the son of Omri began to reign over Israel, and Ahab the son of Omri reigned over Israel in Samaria twenty-two years. And Ahab the son of Omri did evil in the sight of the Lord, more than all who were before him. ESV

Guiding Commentary – Ahab was the son of Omri, the sixth king of the northern kingdom, who gained that throne through political assassination and a coup. So Ahab came from some power hungry stock. And just as we see in some of these kinds of political leaders today, he was badness from badness, as if the sins of the father were passed on. Our scripture identifies Ahab as being the biggest sinner, the most evil king, that the Israelites had ever seen.

What was it that made him so bad? He married an evil woman, Jezebel, who ended up being the perfect partner in crime for Ahab. Together they killed off their political opponents; they did their best to eliminate Yahweh worship by killing off some of His prophets. They raised up hundreds of Baal worshipping priests and celebrated them. They practiced the ritual of infant sacrifice through offering children to Baal. Eventually though God had enough. He sent Elijah to Ahab and told him that He was about to punish Ahab for all his sins by taking his life as well as the life of his wife and kids. (1 Kings 21:17-23) However Ahab repented and God relented for one generation, allowing Ahab to die in battle, but still carried out His promise eventually.

In Christian recovery we often hear stories like Ahab's, maybe not so dramatic, but showing the same patterns. The two primary patterns we run across are the generational pattern and the nuclear family pattern. The first is where we pick up sinful attitudes and behaviors from our family of origin; for example grandparents and parents of alcoholics were often heavy drinkers too. The second occurs when we team up through marriage or friendship with others who are highly dysfunctional which then leads to ongoing problems. This is why part of our moral inventory ought to include an assessment of these two patterns.

<u>The Exercise</u> – Take a look at your family tree, and map it out on paper, go at least as far back as your grandparents. If there have been divorces and remarriages, include those people too. As much as you can build a short profile for each person in your tree, remembering to ask those who are still living for extra information they may have. Look for outward signs of compulsions, such as drinking, heavy smoking, womanizing, dipping snuff, abuse, abandonment etc. When you finish you ought to have a picture of the family dysfunctional history for your recovery records. Next, take a look at all the "friends" you had during your growing up years and your acting out days; build a profile for them too. Include your spouse or spouses.

Go over this part of your inventory with your sponsor or mentor.

Sponsor Notes: _____

_____

_____

Useful Feeling Words:

- Unworthy, Ashamed, Vulnerable, Repentant, Fear

Useful Attitudinal Words:

- Rebellious, Denial, Impulsiveness, Apathetic, Aggravated

My Pre-exercise Notes: _____

_____

_____

_____

The suggested step for Exercise 16 is Step 4.

Exercise 17

1 Kings 18:21

<u>Elijah – Idol Hunter</u>

1 Kings 18:21 - And Elijah came near to all the people and said, "How long will you go limping between two different opinions? If the Lord is God, follow him; but if Baal, then follow him." And the people did not answer him a word. ESV

<u>Guiding Commentary</u> – Elijah is often recognized as one of the great prophets, or spokesmen for God, in the Old Testament. He is highly revered in Jewish extra-biblical writings, and was seen by Peter, James and John during the transfiguration scene in Mark 9. Some even believed that John the Baptist was Elijah come back to life, an example of spiritual wishful thinking.

In this passage (read 1 Kings 18 for the full story) we see Elijah ask a question of the people. How long are you going to be ambivalent? Follow God or follow your idol. And the people did not answer.

In Christian recovery we almost all have to face this question at least once, and some of the more obstinate of us face it several times. God was so faithful to His people, Israel, that He sent prophet after prophet to them to ask basically the same question. "How long are you going to have a foot in both worlds, Mine and your idol's?" He will do the same for us! God will send each of us an Elijah figure, a person who will ask us something or point something out about us having one foot in the camp of God and the other in our compulsions. God describes us as "double-minded" and "unstable" when we are like this. (James 1:8)

<u>The Exercise</u> – Think back over your life, particularly the early part of recovery. Who did God send, who was your Elijah figure? It could be a spouse, a friend, a sponsor, a counselor or even someone you didn't know. You may have had several Elijah figures.

Write about each time you can remember a person coming to you or even accidentally reminding you of your ongoing struggle to get that left foot out of the worldly camp, where you were following some kind of idol. As you write, think back to what you felt or thought and what attitudes you displayed to the message and also the message bearer. What do you think they may have been experiencing as they obeyed God and told you something you didn't want to hear? Do you need to go back to them and thank them for giving you a difficult message?

Are you still struggling with having a foot in God's camp and the other in your compulsions, the camp of the Baals? If we are honest, most of us are. For the final part of this exercise then, write out a prayer asking God to send us an Elijah figure, and asking Him to give us the grace to say thank you when we hear the message we need to hear.

Sponsor Notes: _____

_____

_____

Useful Feeling Words:

- Hurt, Fearful, Ignorant, Enlightened, Optimism

Useful Attitudinal Words:

- Denial, Disobedient, Escapism, Prideful, Embarrassment

My Pre-exercise Notes: _____

_____

_____

_____

_____

The suggested step for Exercise 17 is Step 3.

Exercise 18

Genesis 25:20-21

<u>Rebekah – Conniving Trickster</u>

Gen 25:20-21 - Isaac was forty years old when he took Rebekah to be his wife, the daughter of Bethuel the Aramean of Paddan-aram, the sister of Laban the Aramean. And Isaac prayed to the Lord for his wife, because she was barren. And the Lord granted his prayer, and Rebekah his wife conceived. ESV

<u>Guiding Commentary</u> – When it was time to find a wife for Isaac, Abraham and Sarah sent a servant to Abraham's family of origin. The servant brought back Rebekah who was the sister of Laban, and daughter of Abraham's nephew. Laban becomes a significant figure later in Rebekah's story as his two daughters both marry Rebekah and Isaac's son Jacob.

In this tale of dysfunctional families we see a common thread, a thread of deceit. And it first shows up in Rebekah in the story of tricking Isaac into passing the blessing on to Jacob instead of his older brother Esau. (Gen 27:1-29) There is more trickery from Rebekah as she sends Jacob away to find a wife. Then we see more deceit in her brother Laban and even her son Jacob as the story unfolds. All of this was foreseen by God and He used Rebekah's treachery to bless the world through Jacob and eventually the Messiah, Jesus.

Deceit is the common thread we find in all of our recovery stories. Whether have been deceivers, like Rebekah, or have been deceived by the lies or betrayal of others, we are all touched by deceit. The single biggest area of deceit we see in recovery is that of self-deceit, usually called denial. We deny we have problems, we deny and minimize our dysfunctions and we deny we are hurting ourselves and others.

<u>The Exercise</u> – In this exercise we are going to create a denial inventory by looking at our denials using these three aspects:

1. Denying the reality of the fact. This is normally what most people think of as "denial".
2. Admit the fact, but deny the seriousness of it, we call that minimization.

3. Admit the fact and the seriousness, but deny responsibility, that is called transference or sometimes blaming others.

Take a look at you life's history and pick up to three examples of each of the three types of denial (reality, minimization and transference) described above, for a total of nine examples. Describe the situation and the lie you believed (or told) and mention who was affected or hurt in some way by your denial.

Write a prayer of request to God to open your eyes up to any other denials that linger in your heart, pray it each day for a week.

Sponsor Notes: _____

_____

_____

Useful Feeling Words:

- Confused, Guilty, Exposed, Powerless, Unworthy

Useful Attitudinal Words:

- Disillusioned, Denial, Pessimism, Optimism, Eagerness

My Pre-exercise Notes: _____

_____

_____

_____

_____

The suggested step for Exercise 18 is Step 4.

Exercise 19

John 3:1-2

<u>Nicodemus – Truth Seeker</u>

John 3:1-2 - Now there was a man of the Pharisees named Nicodemus, a ruler of the Jews. This man came to Jesus by night and said to him, "Rabbi, we know that you are a teacher come from God, for no one can do these signs that you do unless God is with him. ESV

<u>Guiding Commentary</u> – Nicodemus is only mentioned in the book of John, where he is called "a ruler of the Jews" a term used for a member of the ruling Jewish council, the Sanhedrin. (Jn 3:1) He is mentioned in only three contexts. The first context, in our focus verses, is when he goes to visit Jesus in secret at night to ask him some questions. The second context is where he comes to Jesus' defense, and gets sarcastically condemned for it. (Jn7:50-52) The last is when he assists physically and financially in the burial of Jesus, a public event that proves he found the truth he was seeking in Jesus. (Jn 19:38-40)

The verses including and after our focus verses record, in my opinion, the single most important conversation recorded in scripture. Read this encounter between Nicodemus and Jesus in Jn 3:1-21, this has been changing lives for two centuries. In this we see the term "born-again" first appear, we see Jesus declare that He must be lifted up, and that He was given by God to save the world through belief in Him.

In Christian recovery we are all truth seekers, we seek the truth about what we have done, who we are and what we must do to move from being ruled by our compulsions to being ruled by Christ. For successful recovery, no matter what our dysfunctional or compulsive behaviors may have been, no matter what we have done or what has been done to us, we must all seek truth, and truth has one source, the God/man Jesus Christ. Just like Nicodemus we must come to Jesus with an open heart seeking truth, for He is God, He designed and created us, and He knows how to heal us.

<u>The Exercise</u> – In this exercise we want to connect with truth searching. First, write a self- assessment of how well you were doing in seeking truth before you

got into recovery. Build your assessment in two parts; truth-seeking in the most common sense, meaning truth found in facts, figures, science and reason, secondly truth found in theological places such as prayer, meditation and bible study. Include references to what you believe your attitudes to truth might have been during this period, and the sources you consulted to learn truth.

Next, write about your truth-seeking activities now; start by reading Jn 8:31-32 and Jn 14:6. Include a statement of what you believe knowing truth will do for you. Finally write a prayer statement about how you intend to seek truth going forward in recovery and pray this for yourself for one week.

Sponsor Notes: _____

_____

_____

Useful Feeling Words:

- Ashamed, Rejected, Fearful, Open, Desirous

Useful Attitudinal Words:

- Truthfulness, Denial, Shamefulness, Vulnerable, Anxiety

My Pre-exercise Notes: _____

_____

_____

_____

_____

The suggested step for Exercise 19 is Step 2.

Exercise 20

Aaron – Approval Addict

Num 20:23-24 - And the Lord said to Moses and Aaron at Mount Hor, on the border of the land of Edom, "Let Aaron be gathered to his people, for he shall not enter the land that I have given to the people of Israel, because you rebelled against my command at the waters of Meribah. ESV

Guiding Commentary – Aaron was Moses' full brother and the first high priest of the nation of Israel. He was also Moses' spokesman (Ex 4:14-16) during the time of the plagues of Egypt as the two of them negotiated the release of the slaves from the Pharaoh. (Ex 5-14)

Aaron was a weak man, from a worldly perspective. But he was still the man God chose to become the high priest and speak the words of God given to him through Moses. And he was just like us! He was an approval addict. Just take a look at what he did in Exodus chapter 32, he allowed himself to be persuaded to make a golden calf, so that the Israelites could worship it. This was amazing because he had just witnessed God's power in the deliverance of His people. On top of this, he exhibited rebellion against God in Numbers 12, and more unbelief in Numbers 16, as mentioned by God in our focus verses. For this last sin, he was prohibited from entering the promised-land, and was even told when and where he would die.

Aaron was a man that needed recovery. He was a believer, but he was fallen and plagued by character defects like all of us in recovery are. God disciplined him again and again until He finally said, "Enough, it is time to come home."

The Exercise – We have a lot to work with here, but we are going to focus on the three main points raised above. Take a look back to your time before recovery and answer the following three questions:

1. Did I seek the approval of others?
2. Was I rebellious toward God and His instructions?
3. How did I exhibit unbelief?

Write two paragraphs for each of the three questions detailing out your answers with specific examples of approval-seeking, rebellion and unbelief. Then discuss this with your spiritual guide.

Note – This could be done as part of your moral inventory or any separate work being done on character defects.

Sponsor Notes: _____

_____

_____

Useful Feeling Words:

- Apprehensive, Grateful, Rebellious, Disbelief, Prideful

Useful Attitudinal Words:

- Prideful, Unworthiness, Pessimistic, Disapproving, Sorrowful

My Pre-exercise Notes: _____

_____

_____

_____

_____

The suggested step for Exercise 20 is Step 4.

Exercise 21

Genesis 49:1-2

Jacob – Defective Inheritor

Gen 49:1-2 - Then Jacob called his sons and said, "Gather yourselves together, that I may tell you what shall happen to you in days to come. Assemble and listen, O sons of Jacob, listen to Israel your father." ESV

Guiding Commentary – There is so much material on Jacob in the Bible, that we can make a really good assessment of his character. He was deceitful, shrewd in business, fearful, compulsively lustful, angry, self-centered, argumentative and more. He was a very flawed individual and yet God chose him to bring forth the twelve tribes of Israel from whom sprang the beginning of the fulfillment of the Abrahamic Covenant (Gen 12:1-3) and ultimately the Messiah, Jesus. It is easy to wonder why God would choose such an imperfect character to be the seed of the promise.

In our focus verses we see Jacob on his death bed about to bless every one of his sons. (Gen 49:1-33) Here we see a man that has changed. He is no longer the disobedient trickster of his youth and early manhood. He has matured to the point where God has trusted him with prophetic words for his sons. He has ceased to walk in his own ways and is walking in God's ways.

For us in Christian recovery Jacob personifies hope and the never ending pursuit that God has for our hearts. Hope because he was like the worst of us, lying, thieving, murdering, sexually immoral, envious and highly dysfunctional, and yet he was able to overcome all of these things to become a godly man. Pursuit because God took him and transformed him day by day into the man God designed and planned for. What is true about Jacob is true for us. God will work with us to develop godly character, and will pursue us until the day we die in His quest to fulfill His plans for us.

The Exercise – This exercise assumes that we have identified at least some of our character defects and are ready to go to God to discuss them with Him.

Collect any work you have done identifying your character defects and read it all. Now write a summarizing list on a single sheet of paper, spend one hour in meditation over it. Next write a prayer that includes at least the following items; thankfulness to God for helping you to identify these defects, a request for God's Spirit to place in you the hope of the magnitude of transformation seen in Jacob's life, an expression of your willingness to accept God's plan for you (no matter what it may be), a request for Him to help you overcome any pride or unbelief that is in you about this subject and a statement of desire to be free from all the character defects that God has helped you identify. Give a copy of your list of defects and your written prayer to three people you trust and ask them to pray it for you each day for a week.

Sponsor Notes: _____

_____

_____

Useful Feeling Words:

- Arrogant, Ashamed, Prideful, Defective, Guilt

Useful Attitudinal Words:

- Prideful, Disobedient, Burdened, Worthlessness, Brokenness

My Pre-exercise Notes: _____

_____

_____

_____

The suggested step for Exercise 21 is Step 7.

Exercise 22

Judges 14:2-3

<u>Samson – Sex Addict</u>

Judg 14:2-3 - Then he came up and told his father and mother, "I saw one of the daughters of the Philistines at Timnah. Now get her for me as my wife." But his father and mother said to him, "Is there not a woman among the daughters of your relatives, or among all our people, that you must go to take a wife from the uncircumcised Philistines?" But Samson said to his father, "Get her for me, for she is right in my eyes." ESV

<u>Guiding Commentary</u> – Samson was most likely the last of the "Judges", individuals raised by God to lead Israel from apostasy back to a right standing. His story is found in Judges 13-16. Samson was a strong man, endowed by God with great physical strength; he was a Nazirite, a man set aside for holy pursuits; but he had a problem with lust and eventually sex addiction.

In this passage we see Samson's lust and sexual compulsion appear for the first time. Look at what he says, "She is right in my eyes." (see Pr 3:7 and 12:15) Today he would be sitting in front of a computer starring at porn, going to "gentleman's clubs" and hiring call girls! Samson married several times, had concubines and eventually became so consumed by his sexual needs that he gave away his relationship with God as he pursued Delilah, the Philistine temptress. (Judg 16:4-21) This resulted in his capture and enslavement by the enemy of Israel; they gouged his eyes out, the very organ that he used to look at the objects of his lust, and made him work like an ox. Ultimately, he came back to God, but the whole sorry episode cost him his physical life.

If anyone reads this and because they don't act out sexually believe it doesn't apply to them, they are missing the point. With Samson, the whole problem is obvious. With us today, no matter if we are men or women, we are all plagued with sexual temptation. And, although most of us may not admit it, sexual lust lurks in the deep recesses of our mind.

<u>The Exercise</u> – This is a simple exercise, but one an unseasoned person will have trouble with. Go back to your earliest memories of when you were attracted to

another person. This can be opposite or same-gender attraction. Was sexual lust part of your attraction? Write down in one paragraph your memories of this attraction and any sexual content that was involved. If you took the attraction from the lust stage to acting out sexually, record this in your paragraph. Do this for up to 10 people in your life before you entered recovery. Then write one paragraph on any patterns you see in these stories. If you are struggling with this in any way, such as remembering, unwillingness to confess, unbelief that you deal with sexual lust, then you must pray before you start.

Share the results of this exercise with your sponsor and/or counselor.

Sponsor Notes: _____

_____

_____

Useful Feeling Words:

- Isolated, Rejected, Worthless, Ashamed, Guilt

Useful Attitudinal Words:

- Temptation, Bitterness, Hopelessness, Pain, Disbelieving

My Pre-exercise Notes: _____

_____

_____

_____

The suggested step for Exercise 22 is Step 10.

Exercise 23

Jeremiah 1:11-12

Jeremiah – Called Newbie

Jer 1:11-12 - And the word of the Lord came to me, saying, "Jeremiah, what do you see?" And I said, "I see an almond branch." Then the Lord said to me, "You have seen well, for I am watching over my word to perform it." ESV

<u>Guiding Commentary</u> – Jeremiah, whom I have named here "Called Newbie", is usually known as the weeping prophet. He was one of the Major Prophets given by God to the Israelites, and carried warnings of doom and gloom, from their perspective. In his two books, Jeremiah and Lamentations, he tells us a lot about himself. He was called as a teenager, possibly at age 19, and suffered much from a psychological perspective. He and his message were constantly rejected, and he fell into deep depressions throughout his life.

In the scene we see through our focus verses Jeremiah is still in the middle of the moment when God called him. He has just been told he is going to be a big time messenger for God, and this scene happens. God asks Jeremiah what he saw, we don't know if it was his first vision, but it seems to be. A branch of an almond tree, Jeremiah says. God says yes, this is because I am going to make sure My word (warnings in this case) get out and will be done. The almond tree is one of the first trees each year to blossom and produce its harvest. Aaron's rod (Num 17) the symbol of God's divine appointment and sometimes thought of as the rod of discipline was made from almond wood. Jeremiah was going to be used as God's disciplining agent.

In Christian recovery we see people who are God's disciplining agents. Being a disciplining agent is not a pleasant task because messages have to be delivered that are not well accepted. Sometimes these things result in individual rejection, as happened with Jeremiah. Any one of us can be called to bring a message of God to a recovery fellowship or an individual. The person called may have one day, one year or ten years of recovery experience. None of us needs to become so complacent or arrogant in our recovery as to reject a message of discipline. How do we recognize a message? It is something that makes us uncomfortable. Take care of the messengers, they have enormous value!

<u>The Exercise</u> – Write about your experiences of hearing messages delivered by others in your recovery group. You may have been sitting quietly and somebody shared something which hit you, you may have been directly spoken to or the group topic possibly caught you off guard. Think back and pick three to five such incidents, as you describe them include some words on if you recognized that God was speaking to you through others. Next, write about the possibility that you may have been called to deliver messages of discipline, or that you know you are already called. As you do this remember that such messages don't all have to be doom and gloom, they can be uplifting too. Write about any fear of rejection you may be anticipating or have experienced.

Sponsor Notes: _____

_____

_____

Useful Feeling Words:

- Excited, Unworthy, Apprehensive, Scared, Worried

Useful Attitudinal Words:

- Humble, Optimistic, Surprised, Amiable, Eagerness

My Pre-exercise Notes: _____

_____

_____

_____

The suggested step for Exercise 23 is Step 11.

Exercise 24

Job 42:1-2, 6

<u>Job - Godly Self-Despiser</u>

Job 42:1-2, 6 - Then Job answered the Lord and said: "I know that you can do all things, and that no purpose of yours can be thwarted. V6 Therefore I despise myself, and repent in dust and ashes." ESV

<u>Guiding Commentary</u> – Job was a rich man, much blessed by God, and by the devil's hand he lost everything except his wife. His real estate, his livestock, his personal health and most significantly his children were all taken from him. As he has to deal with his grief we see him get advice from his wife to "curse God and die" (Job 2:9) which he did not do, he maintained his spiritual integrity (Job 2:10).

The tale of Job is one of the most intriguing stories in scripture. From Job 3 to Job 37 we see Job dialoging with his friends, then God steps in with a great question in Job 38; I'm going to paraphrase here, "Who do you think you are?" God speaks for four chapters and finally Job responds with our focus verses.

One of the truths about those in recovery is that they have had great losses. In fact we ought to fully embrace that the word recovery is short for "recovery from personal losses." Probably the big three things we have lost are material wealth, relationships and integrity. In doing this we may have left a trail of destruction behind us. And it is our best thinking that got us into this position. That is why we must get to the same point that Job did. We must recognize that God can do all things for us; and that we must despise ourselves and repent. Do not misunderstand what "despise" means here; it is the Hebrew word "**ma'ac**" meaning to disappear something. Just as it says all through the New Testament, we (our inner selfish person) are to lessen and God is to increase in our lives. That is the path to unshakable recovery!

<u>The Exercise</u> – It may be helpful to read the whole book of Job with recovery eyes before doing this exercise, or at least Job 1-3 and Job 38-42.

Write about your spiritual journey in recovery. Start with how you lived a self-centered life, a life which excluded God, even though you may have gone to church, bible study or engaged in other spiritual disciplines. Try to provide a written expression of how spiritual you really were. Next talk about how your awareness of your powerlessness over life has grown, and where you are now. Talk about the impact that confessing God's way (James 5:16) has had on you, if you engaged in a step program talk a little about going through step 4 and 5. Finally, write about where you are today in your relationship with God, including words on seeking his will, trusting Him and being obedient to His instructions. Go through all this with your spiritual advisor.

Sponsor Notes: _____

_____

_____

Useful Feeling Words:

- Selfish, Guilt, Mistrusting, Powerless, Pride

Useful Attitudinal Words:

- Worthlessness, Inadequacy, Self-centered, Disgusted, Apathetic

My Pre-exercise Notes: _____

_____

_____

_____

_____

The suggested step for Exercise 24 is Step 11.

Exercise 25

2 Samuel 13:1-2

<u>Amnon – Family Rapist</u>

2 Sam 13:1-2 - Now Absalom, David's son, had a beautiful sister, whose name was Tamar. And after a time Amnon, David's son, loved her. And Amnon was so tormented that he made himself ill because of his sister Tamar, for she was a virgin, and it seemed impossible to Amnon to do anything to her. ESV

<u>Guiding Commentary</u> – Amnon, translated by some as "my mother is the serpent", was the crown prince of Israel, the heir to the throne of David. Amnon seems to have inherited his father's lust problem, and was just as weak as David in not handling it. David had his way with Bathsheba (2 Sam 11) and later in this story Amnon raped his half-sister Tamar (2 Sam 13:14). Ultimately it resulted in Absalom killing his half brother (2 Sam 13:28-29), the fleeing of Absalom from the court and the initiation of a big family feud.

While this story of the highly dysfunctional first family of Israel would provide us with some great material for a modern day soap opera, it has a serious point to make. This whole chain of events was begun when Amnon could not deal with his lust in healthy way. He told his friend, Jonadab, about it and instead of getting good counsel about staying away from the high temptation, his "friend" showed Amnon a way to get his evil desires satiated.

In this entire story we see lust being the beginning of evil at work. We see ungodly advice, immoral friends, rape, depression of the victim, murder, lots of lying and the breakup of a family. More comes later, but I think the point is made, unbridled lust can lead to dark, dark places. This is why Jesus rightly told us to watch out for it in Mt 5:27-28.

<u>The Exercise</u> – In 1 Jn 2:16 the Apostle identifies the three big lusts that all of us are subject to. I'm going to paraphrase them; the lust of the eyes, the lust of the flesh and the lust for possessions.

To start this exercise get a notepad and at the top write "my historical lust examples", then section the first page into three columns; Eyes, Flesh, and Things.

Then get quiet and search your memory for anything that God brings up for you in any of these areas. Sit like this for as long as you can, and start to list them. As you write one down add to it some key words like the name of a person, place or time. Do this once a day for a week and accumulate your historical lust inventory. From this inventory pick a total of five items, with at least one from each column, and journal about it; the details, the things, people, places, times, severity, how it led your behavior and the results of letting it get the better of you.

After this, do a current lust inventory. What kind of lusts are you dealing with now, and how are you handling them. Discuss all this with your sponsor or other spiritual advisor.

Sponsor Notes: _____

_____

_____

Useful Feeling Words:

- Sorry, Regret, Ashamed, Guilty, Humiliated

Useful Attitudinal Words:

- Helplessness, Powerlessness, Brokenness, Humbled, Sorrowful

My Pre-exercise Notes: _____

_____

_____

_____

_____

The suggested step for Exercise 25 is Step 4.

Exercise 26

Matthew 4:21-22

<u>Zebedee – Sacrificing Father</u>

Matt 4:21-22 - And going on from there he saw two other brothers, James the son of Zebedee and John his brother, in the boat with Zebedee their father, mending their nets, and he called them. Immediately they left the boat and their father and followed him. ESV

<u>Guiding Commentary</u> – Zebedee, which is a name rooted in the Hebrew word "zebed" meaning gift (as in a dowry), is often viewed as meaning "gift of God" by translators. This is significant in this passage. Zebedee is pictured as a man of some means (Mk 1:20) because he could afford to hire servants, maybe he is best thought of a businessman. He and his family seemed to know the high priest of Israel (Jn 18:15), meaning he was also likely to be a man of influence, probably religious, and perhaps he was not only a businessman, but an early version of a political lobbyist.

In our focus verses we see him getting his hands dirty with his two sons, James and John, by mending nets. Jesus comes by and calls James and John to ministry. The scripture here says that James and John, destined to be disciples and then Apostles, immediately left the boat, and the job they were doing with their father, Zebedee, to accept the call. Being young men from a good family, James and John (who it is believed may have been a teenager) most likely turned to their father, Zebedee and asked if it was okay. Zebedee made a singular and life changing choice and said yes to God, by releasing his two sons to Jesus for an unknown calling. Compare this to the calling of Isaiah in Isa 6:8, where immediacy is also found.

In Christ-centered recovery people are also called. All are called, like James and John, to follow Jesus, give, give back, serve and use their personal gifts and talents for the building of God's kingdom. Some are called to lead, teach or mentor, and be God's representative in the holy work of helping the down and out and broken-hearted. If God calls us, are we going to immediately say yes, like James and John did, are we going to sacrifice something like Zebedee did?

<u>The Exercise</u> – Write a paragraph on each of the following statements about your calling:

- How I am called to follow Jesus.
- How I am called to give to the kingdom of God in recovery.
- How I am called to give back to my recovery fellowship.
- How I am called to serve God through recovery.
- How I can use my gifts and talents in recovery.
- How I am to sacrifice in recovery.

The purpose of this exercise is to be clear about how we are personally called.

Sponsor Notes: _____

_____

_____

Useful Feeling Words:

- Glad, Uplifted, Excited, Apprehensive, Happy

Useful Attitudinal Words:

- Sacrificial, Relentlessness, Joyful, Fearful, Expectant

My Pre-exercise Notes: _____

_____

_____

_____

_____

The suggested step for Exercise 26 is Step 12.

Exercise 27

Joshua 2:3-4(a)

<u>Rahab – Godly Prostitute</u>

Josh 2:3-4(a) - Then the king of Jericho sent to Rahab, saying, "Bring out the men who have come to you, who entered your house, for they have come to search out all the land." But the woman had taken the two men and hidden them. ESV

<u>Guiding Commentary</u> – Rahab is a very interesting character. Traditionally she is posited as a prostitute, and sometimes as an innkeeper. Extra biblical Jewish writings have named her as a wife of Joshua. Hebrews 11:31 says she was a prostitute saved by faith, which is why I've called her a godly prostitute. James uses her as an example of being justified by works. (Jas 2:25) Most importantly, Rahab is mentioned in the lineage of Jesus in Mt 1:5.

In the story (Josh 2:1-21) Rahab, because she came to a saving faith through fear of God due to what He was doing with the nation of Israel, hides two spies sent to check out Jericho. She unknowingly becomes part of God's plan to destroy Jericho, and even more, becomes part of God's eternal plan to save the human race. She saved the life of the two spies, and as a reward, her family alone survived the destruction of Jericho.

Symbolically, she is told to hang a scarlet thread out of the window of her home so that the Israelites can identify her household and not destroy it. Today, thousands of years later, we know that the scarlet thread was a foreshadowing of the blood of Christ, shed to save us all.

This story, if we appreciate the spiritual lessons in it, can really enhance the outcome of our Christ-centered recovery program. It helps us to focus on the truth that Christ saves us, helps to clean us up, and gives us an opportunity to respond to Him.

<u>The Exercise</u> – At the end of a program it is time to sit and meditate on all that Christ has done for us, and how we are going to respond.

The exercise is simply to think back over one's time in recovery, and journal what we know or understand that Christ has done for us through our program, and through the people He put into our lives. Write it all down, in summary form; acknowledge everything you can remember He has accomplished in you, and name all the people who He has put in your life for the season you've been in recovery. Write out a prayer of thanks.

Next, meditate on the question, "How am I going to respond to what Christ has done for me?" After a reasonable time period, which may be a few days, write your promise to God, and to your recovery fellowship of how you are going to serve Christ as part of your grateful response. Note that you may not be asked by God to serve the fellowship, it could be service elsewhere.

Sponsor Notes: _____

_____

_____

Useful Feeling Words:

- Happy, Glad, Meditative, Confident, Reverent

Useful Attitudinal Words:

- Accepting, Contentment, Hopefulness, Expectant, Brave

My Pre-exercise Notes: _____

_____

_____

_____

The suggested step for Exercise 27 is Step 12.

Exercise 28

2 Kings 20:1

Hezekiah – Prideful King

2 Kings 20:1 - In those days Hezekiah became sick and was at the point of death. And Isaiah the prophet the son of Amoz came to him and said to him, "Thus says the Lord, 'Set your house in order, for you shall die; you shall not recover. ESV

Guiding Commentary – Hezekiah is pictured in scripture as one of the most godly kings of Judah, the southern kingdom. He reigned for 29 years, and brought reformation to the nation. He reopened the temple, cleansed the nation of idols and reestablished Yahweh worship.

Hezekiah was faced with treachery from Sennacherib, king of Assyria, who invaded Judah a second time, even after being bought off with a tribute. Hezekiah and Isaiah prayed "and cried to Heaven" about this siege. (2 Chron 32:20) God in response slew the entire Assyrian army of 185,000 men, and Sennacherib went back to Assyria in disgrace, where he was assassinated by his sons. (2 Chron 32:21) Then we see Hezekiah start to believe that he was the one who made this all happen, read 2 Chron 32:20-26. This is when God sent Isaiah to tell Hezekiah that he was going to die, as described in our focus verse. Hezekiah repented of his pride, and God delayed his judgment for another 15 years. (2 Kings 20:4-6)

One of the greatest things we discover in Christian recovery is how pride has impacted us. We eventually come to acknowledge that pride was part of the reason we acted out. We also realize that pride is still an ongoing problem as we work our programs, and that pride is likely to be a "thorn in our flesh" (2 Cor 12:7) for the rest of our lives. At some level we must all end up agreeing with the statement, "My pride is unjustifiable in the context of my beliefs and the Holy One I serve, and I must guard my heart from it and its effects in my life."

The Exercise – Part of our spiritual inventory ought to be a thorough and detailed look at pride in our lives. If you haven't done this, then go back to the inventory and add it. We recommend that you simply look at five life situations from pre-recovery days, describe them and detail how pride (Inordinate and unjustifiable self-esteem) was part of the reason you acted out.

If you have done this, or when you complete it, then write out a prayer having these elements; confession and repentance about your pride, a statement that you don't want pride to be part of your character and a request to God to discipline you if you ever become prideful.

Lastly, go to a safe place and spend time with God, praying your prayer, and make amends with God for all of your pridefulness. Allow Him to speak to you during this time, and record in your personal journal anything you believe God shares with you.

Sponsor Notes: _____

_____

_____

Useful Feeling Words:

- Prideful, Cautious, Arrogant, Afraid, Ashamed

Useful Attitudinal Words:

- Stubbornness, Negative, Arrogance, Self-centered, Rebelliousness

My Pre-exercise Notes: _____

_____

_____

_____

The suggested step for Exercise 28 is Step 9.

Exercise 29

Genesis 50:19-20

Joseph – Life Saver

Gen 50:19-20 - But Joseph said to them, "Do not fear, for am I in the place of God? As for you, you meant evil against me, but God meant it for good, to bring it about that many people should be kept alive, as they are today. ESV

Guiding Commentary – Joseph is one of the great figures of scripture, and is often revered in Christian literature as a type of Christ. However, Joseph was a pesky little sibling. He was father's favorite (Gen 37:3); smart, good looking, virtuous and very annoying. He told his brothers a dream in Gen 37:5-8 to which the brothers responded by selling him into slavery.

In our focus scripture we see Joseph speaking to God's purpose in the dream he told, in his slavery, in his imprisonment and finally in his ascension to power in Egypt. He points out to the very people that sold him into slavery that although their actions were evil and meant to harm him, God had other plans. Joseph shares a simple truth that is true today. God can take the evil in our lives and turn it to good. And sometimes that good saves lives.

We see this so often in recovery, that our stories have value in the lives of others. Some of our stories literally save others from death, some from imprisonment, and some from staying in the death spiral of addiction. We see that the evil we have done, or has been done to us is used by God to bring strength, courage and hope into the lives of many people.

The Exercise – In this exercise we want to consider the idea of a personal story. First think of the names of two or three people who have influenced you in recovery through their story. Write your memory of their story in one paragraph, including how it influenced you, highlight any evil in their story, and any good, as evidence that God was at work in their lives.

Next, write out a short version of your story, maybe up to three paragraphs so that it can be told in five minutes or less. Include the evidence of evil, good and God's hand at work in your life through it. Discuss this with your spiritual advisor, and with him or her, tweak it as necessary, and do your best to memorize it

Now find three people who are new to recovery and either read it to them or speak it from memory. Ask them for immediate feedback. Continue on into a dialog if the conversation goes that way. Discuss the story telling with your spiritual advisor; how it went, how you felt, how confident you were and what kind of feedback you got.

Finally spend some time in prayer after it is all over asking God to bring you people who would benefit from hearing your story, and to help keep you ready to share it.

Sponsor Notes: _____

_____

_____

Useful Feeling Words:

- Encouraged, Built-up, Down-trodden, Apprehensive, Guilty

Useful Attitudinal Words:

- Hopelessness, Powerlessness, Unworthiness, Positive, Negative

My Pre-exercise Notes: _____

_____

_____

_____

The suggested step for Exercise 29 is Step 5.

Exercise 30

Hosea 1:2-3

Hosea – Suffering Husband

Hos 1:2-3 - When the Lord first spoke through Hosea, the Lord said to Hosea, "Go, take to yourself a wife of whoredom and have children of whoredom, for the land commits great whoredom by forsaking the Lord." So he went and took Gomer, the daughter of Diblaim, and she conceived and bore him a son. ESV

Guiding Commentary – It is not easy being a prophet, and Hosea can testify strongly to this. This poor guy was told by God to take a prostitute, Gomer, as a wife, and to have children by her. God's purpose was the same as it always was with prophets, to reveal to Israel their sin and apostasy, followed by statements of coming judgments, and usually followed by God's plan of redemption.

The story of the unfortunate Hosea and his wayward wife is one of betrayal where God parallels the sins of Israel and the sins of Gomer. He calls His people whores through this prophet and admonishes them over and over again to turn away from their sin, mostly idol worship, and to come back to Him.

Some of us were thrown into recovery by our own Gomers, people who betrayed us. They may have been sexually or emotionally unfaithful, they may have drunk, drugged or gambled our money away, they may have sucked us emotionally dry through their co-dependency or they may simply be those demanding perfectionists, the people who demand everything from you and who we can never please. The story of Hosea is just for you; it shows how God empathizes and knows just what you have been through.

The Exercise – If you are in a program of recovery ostensibly because of the actions of another person, you are not alone! Many of us found our way here because of others. This exercise focuses of the actions of others.

Write out your version of the circumstances that surround you getting into recovery. Then add to it a statement that identifies what you thought and felt at the time. Did you enter recovery unwillingly? Now move forward in time; when did you first realize that you were really in recovery for yourself and not for any person who pushed you into it? Write about that journey of discovery.

Now, the hard part! Can you honestly say that you are grateful for being pushed into recovery, while not being grateful for the circumstances that caused it? If your answer is yes, write out a prayer of thanks to God for you being able to be in recovery, and for all those who are helping you (name them). If your answer is no, write out a prayer of petition to God to change your heart to fully embrace whatever He has for you in your program.

Sponsor Notes: _____

_____

_____

Useful Feeling Words:

- Powerless, Thankful, Encouraged, Stimulated, Cheerful

Useful Attitudinal Words:

- Gratefulness, Courageous, Appreciative, Excitement, Positive

My Pre-exercise Notes: _____

_____

_____

_____

The suggested step for Exercise 30 is Step 5.

Exercise 31

Hosea 3:1-4

Gomer – Symbollic Whore

Hos 3:1-4 - And the Lord said to me, "Go again, love a woman who is loved by another man and is an adulteress, even as the Lord loves the children of Israel, though they turn to other gods and love cakes of raisins." So I bought her for fifteen shekels of silver and a homer and a lethech of barley. And I said to her, "You must dwell as mine for many days. You shall not play the whore, or belong to another man; so will I also be to you." ESV

Guiding Commentary – Gomer is the woman that God told Hosea the prophet to take as a wife. The problem is that she was a prostitute, and not only that she seemed to want to be in that lifestyle. In our focus verse we see that Hosea has to go back and buy her out of the slavery of prostitution again.

Gomer represents all of us! We have all chosen to be spiritual whores, driven by our sinful nature. Recovery for us then is a path of redemption out of our own whoredom, with the power to get out of our compulsions or addictions coming from God.

If you care to read the whole book (14 chapters) with recovery eyes, you will see yourself, as I did. But recovery eyes also show us something else. It is as if the nation of Israel has gone to God to make amends, and God wants to tell them His version of what they have done, before He forgives them. If you've ever made amends you know that this happens. At least one of those people you want to say sorry to wants to have a form of confession of what, in their eyes, you have done to them, sometimes they accept your "sorry", sometimes not. Let us all remember that God will always accept our sincere sorry.

The Exercise – First, write a paragraph or two about your view on being a spiritual whore.

If you are in a program of recovery, at some point you will have gone to those you have hurt to make amends. Some of these individuals have been totally gracious, some have wanted to reestablish relationship with you, and some have totally rejected your overtures and won't even talk to you. Some have forgiven you, some have not. And some have wanted to have their say about what you did to them, often giving it to you with both barrels.

Write about your experiences in making amends, <u>particularly focusing on how you felt</u> during the process of doing it. Take your top ten amendees and without naming names, talk about who wanted to be back in relationship, who didn't, who wanted to forgiving and who didn't, talk about the people who wanted to rehash every event, and talk about any surprises you had.

Sponsor Notes: _____

_____

_____

Useful Feeling Words:

- Fearful, Hurt, Shame, Guilty, Convicted

Useful Attitudinal Words:

- Prideful, Forgiving, Denial, Nervous, Regretful

My Pre-exercise Notes: _____

_____

_____

_____

_____

The suggested step for Exercise 31 is Step 9.

Exercise 32

1 Samuel 1:4-7(a)

<u>Hannah – Faithful Intercessor</u>

1 Sam 1:4-7(a) - On the day when Elkanah sacrificed, he would give portions to Peninnah his wife and to all her sons and daughters. But to Hannah he gave a double portion, because he loved her, though the Lord had closed her womb. And her rival used to provoke her grievously to irritate her, because the Lord had closed her womb. So it went on year by year. ESV

<u>Guiding Commentary</u> – Hannah, which means grace in Hebrew, was one of two wives to Elkanah who was a religious man, and she had not been able to conceive. The ability to bear children was a matter of significance to women in that culture, and Hannah suffered for many years in her barrenness. The other wife, Peninnah, was fruitful and used this fact to taunt Hannah as shown in our story. After this scene Hannah separated herself and spent time with the Lord pouring out her heart (read 1 Sam 1:1-20). She prayed for a child, and in due time, a male child called Samuel was born. After he was weaned, probably about age 4 in that time, he was taken to the temple and dedicated to the Lord and was left under the care of Eli the high priest. This was a promise that Hannah had made to God during her prayer time as she asked for a child. Hannah went on to have 5 other children.

In recovery we sometimes have "dry spells" where we feel barrenness, and we ought to respond to it just as Hannah did, by spending significant time in prayer for God to provide.

<u>The Exercise</u> – Read Hannah's prayer found in 1 Sam 2:1-10. Consult with any commentaries or individuals you know might be able to help with your understanding of the prayer.

Now write a prayer in your own words, that uses Hannah's prayer as a model, about you, your recovery and God. Share it with at least your sponsor, and any other people you believe would understand your heart in it.

Here is the model to use. Verse 1 – Rejoice in God, 2 – lift up your view of God's holiness, 3- lift up your view of God's wisdom, 4 – lift up your view of God's strength, 5 – lift up your view of God's providence, 6 – lift up your view of God's authority over life and death, 7 - lift up your view of God's material provision, 8 – lift up your view of how God raises the least up in life, 9 – lift up your view of His protection, and 10 - lastly lift up your view of what God might do to your adversaries. Remember that this does not have to be perfect! This prayer will be yours, and God will accept it just the way you write it.

After you have finished this, pray it out loud for a week and before sharing it, journal how you felt writing it, praying it and how you feel now that the exercise is done.

Sponsor Notes: _____

_____

_____

Useful Feeling Words:

- Thankful, Encouraged, Expectant, Humble, Serious

Useful Attitudinal Words:

- Gratefulness, Positive, Optimistic, Joyful, Encouraged

My Pre-exercise Notes: _____

_____

_____

_____

The suggested step for Exercise 32 is Step 11.

Exercise 33

Esther 1:16

Vashti – Prideful Rebel

Est 1:16 - Then Memucan said in the presence of the king and the officials, "Not only against the king has Queen Vashti done wrong, but also against all the officials and all the peoples who are in all the provinces of King Ahasuerus. ESV

Guiding Commentary – In the story of Esther, we see this character Queen Vashti, the wife of King Ahasuerus (Xerxes). Vashti was a beautiful woman (Est 1:11), and the king was having a seven day feast for all the people to celebrate the splendor of Persia. The Queen was also having a seven day feast with the royal women. Xerxes wanted Vashti to join him and sent his seven top officials to get her. She refused to come and treated her husband with massive disrespect in front of everybody in town.

From the responses of Xerxes and his officials we can see that this was not a simple no. This was a public rebellion, borne out of pride. The king's officials responded to an angry king with a reasonable observation. If she gets away with this then all the women will become contemptuous of their husbands and we'll have anarchy. Ultimately Xerxes divorced Vashti, and issued an edict that made life more difficult for women in his kingdom. Read the whole story in Est 1:10-22.

How does this fit into Christian recovery? It is a common theme in recovery stories that when we acted out we were being prideful and rebellious. We were going to do things our own way, and nobody, not our friends, bosses, teachers, spouses and especially not God was going to tell us what to do. Our prideful hearts deceived us, and we fell into the great trap of pride, that we think we know better than everybody else. In the end, we make life worse for us, and those around us, notably the people we say we love.

The Exercise – On a single sheet write "Pride Inventory" at the top. Create 4 columns, What I should have done, what I did do, who I hurt and what eventually happened (final outcome). Proceed to list all the rebellious actions you have taken that you can remember from your life. If you fill the page add a new one. Do this only in summary form.

Next take the most egregious five of these and write out a detailed description of them. Focus on what you can remember about what was happening in your life, what you were feeling, thinking and what your attitudes were.

Finally, read over what you have written, and see if you can see any attitudinal patterns of thinking and choosing you have demonstrated. Discuss this pride inventory with your sponsor or other spiritual advisor.

Sponsor Notes: _____

_____

_____

Useful Feeling Words:

- Arrogance, Troubled, Pessimistic, Fearful, Unsafe

Useful Attitudinal Words:

- Fearful, Punishment, Shaming, Willing, Safety

My Pre-exercise Notes: _____

_____

_____

_____

_____

The suggested step for Exercise 33 is Step 4.

Exercise 34

John 20:27-29

Thomas – Disbelieving Believer

John 20:27-29 - Then he said to Thomas, "Put your finger here, and see my hands; and put out your hand, and place it in my side. Do not disbelieve, but believe." Thomas answered him, "My Lord and my God!" Jesus said to him, "Have you believed because you have seen me? Blessed are those who have not seen and yet have believed." ESV

Guiding Commentary – Thomas was the disciple who said he wouldn't believe Jesus was alive after the resurrection unless he personally put his finger on Jesus wounds. He was also the one that Jesus was talking to when He said, "I am the way, the truth and the life." (Jn 14:6) Little else is known about Thomas from the scriptural records. Some apocryphal literature has him dying at the hands of the king of India, where he is thought to have served his mission time.

Thomas represents all of us. In our story we see that he obstinately said I won't believe until I get concrete evidence, so that I can see with my own eyes and feel with my own hands. Jesus graciously chastises him about his unbelief. And then Jesus says words for us down the ages, "Blessed are those who have not seen and yet believed." Almost all of us will not see Jesus until we get to heaven. We are asked by scripture and the Holy Spirit to believe even though we have not seen, and if we choose to do this we will be blessed in some way.

This is so important for us in recovery to understand. God wants us to accept, believe that He is going to help us in our recovery, even though we cannot see, hear or touch Him directly. It is a deep scriptural principle that unbelief is a barrier to healing, or in our case recovery. God asks us not to just believe in Him, but to believe Him. When we only believe in Him, we often reject His instructions and go our own way. When we believe Him, we accept His instructions, and even if we have reservations or resistance inside us, we still obey. That is the path to healing and recovery that God prescribes for us.

The Exercise – This is an opportunity to address a fundamental issue in recovery. Begin by writing, as truthfully as you can, what you believe about Christ and what you anticipate He is going to do for you in your recovery. Next write about what you expect your part in your recovery to be, be as specific as possible, including descriptions of the attitudes you will bring to the table. Then write about what resources God is bringing to you to help you get through recovery, include here a statement acknowledging that you cannot do this recovery thing alone.

Now write about the barriers you expect to encounter, such as things inside you and other people. Lastly write a prayer for yourself about removing all traces of disbelief in God, His ways and His healing power from your inner person.

Sponsor Notes: _____

_____

_____

Useful Feeling Words:

- Believing, Nervous, Encouraged, Ready, Willing

Useful Attitudinal Words:

- Impatience, Afraid, Expectant, Resentment, Optimism

My Pre-exercise Notes: _____

_____

_____

_____

_____

The suggested step for Exercise 34 is Step 3.

Exercise 35

Ezekiel 24:15-16

Ezekiel – Willing Loser

Ezek 24:15-16 - The word of the Lord came to me: "Son of man, behold, I am about to take the delight of your eyes away from you at a stroke; yet you shall not mourn or weep, nor shall your tears run down." ESV

Guiding Commentary – Ezekiel, called "Son of man" here and often in his writings, was one of the major prophets of the Hebrew scriptures. In Ezek 1:3 we see him called a priest also. At the time of his calling to prophesy he lived with some of the Babylonian captives north of Babylon in Chedar. He is also the writer of some of the most important end-times prophecies (Ezek 35-38) and he is the one who saw the valley of dry bones raised by God (Ezek 37:1-14).

In our focus verses we see Ezekiel being told he is going to lose "the delight of his eyes", his wife, to death, and that he is not allowed to grieve for her. In the verses that follow we see that God is speaking to the captives that this death of a beloved wife is symbolic of the Israelites losing Jerusalem to complete destruction, which occurred 3 years later. They were not allowed to grieve this enormous catastrophe, just as Ezekiel was not allowed to grieve the loss of his wife. The destruction of Jerusalem was to be allowed by God as a disciplining action for the nation of Israel who were apostate again. God says this to Ezekiel later, "So you will be a sign to them, and they will know that I am the Lord." (ESV)

In Christian recovery we often hear stories of people's misfortunes, bad luck, negative karma or something equally foolishly interpreted. Sometimes blame is thrown around, and responsibility for our own difficult situations is denied by us as we ignorantly assume that we can actually control our lives if other people would just not mess up. Often the reality is much less palatable, it is not bad luck, nor others that create our problems; things always happen for a reason, and we are often responsible. The good news is that God will exercise His sovereign privilege to discipline us through our circumstances. This demonstrates how great a love He has for His children, which is that He won't let us stay in our dysfunctions.

The Exercise – Take a look back at your life and document all the losses you can identify in a list format. Then classify each one as something that occurred for one of these three reasons; I did it, someone did it to me or the world did it. (Examples are "I drank too much and wrecked my truck", "I was abused" and "I lost my job".) Then pray and ask God to reveal if He used any of these things to discipline you, remembering that He did not cause any of these things to happen.

Now comes the more difficult part of this exercise. Look at what is going on in your life today, particularly the troublesome things, and ask God through prayer and meditation to reveal if He is disciplining you. Journal your sense of what God may be speaking to, and discuss this with your sponsor or other spiritual advisor.

Sponsor Notes: _____

_____

_____

Useful Feeling Words:

- Grief, Guilt, Shame, Thoughtful, Numb

Useful Attitudinal Words:

- Fearful, Passive, Calm, Brave, Confident

My Pre-exercise Notes: _____

_____

_____

_____

_____

The suggested step for Exercise 35 is Step 11.

Exercise 36

Philemon 10-12

Onesimus – Repentant Slave

Philem 10-12 - I appeal to you for my child, Onesimus, whose father I became in my imprisonment. (Formerly he was useless to you, but now he is indeed useful to you and to me.) I am sending him back to you, sending my very heart. ESV

Guiding Commentary – Onesimus was a slave of Philemon, a wealthy man from Colossae, who had run away after defrauding his master in some way. Here Paul refers to Onesimus as his child, meaning his child in the faith, that indicated that Onesimus had become a Christian. Paul, writing from home imprisonment in Rome, beseeches his friend Philemon to take Onesimus back and says to charge his (Paul's) account for any costs. (Philem 17-19) Paul urges Philemon not to take Onesimus back as a slave, but as a brother in Christ. Onesimus is going back to the scene of the crime to make amends to his master.

In our focus verses we see this incredibly important statement; "formerly he was useless to you, but now he is indeed useful to you and to me." Before his conversion to Christianity, he was merely a slave, an indentured servant, who could not be trusted by his master. Now Onesimus has placed himself under God, and therefore Paul and Philemon can both use him in their evangelism. Onesimus has become "useful" most likely because of his story; his Christian witness of how he came to Christ and how Christ has changed him.

The book of Philemon is so rich for us in Christian recovery. We see Onesimus going to make amends; this was no small thing to do, for Philemon could have Onesimus executed for stealing. We see a grateful person, Onesimus, serving the Lord as a result of being saved. We see Paul extending forgiveness to Onesimus and reminding his friend Philemon to do the same. Finally we see Onesimus, formerly a slave to sin, become a slave to Christ.

The Exercise – This exercise is meant to be done when entering the amends phase of a Christ-centered recovery program. Write about your thoughts and feelings about making amends to those you have wronged. Particularly describe any sense of fear, or even terror, about doing this, and also include a confession of any behaviors you are engaging in that are causing you to put off this important activity. Be thorough, this may take up a couple of pages of your recovery journal.

Next write about the level of confidence you have in the amends making process, followed by an honest statement about your belief level that God will see you through this.

As a bonus part of this exercise, write a letter like the one to Philemon, with you being Onesimus, your sponsor being Paul and a person of importance to you that you have to make amends to being Philemon.

Sponsor Notes: _____

_____

_____

Useful Feeling Words:

- Afraid, Apprehensive, Avoidant, Careful, Shame

Useful Attitudinal Words:

- Fearful, Resentment, Anxious, Pessimistic, Somber

My Pre-exercise Notes: _____

_____

_____

_____

_____

The suggested step for Exercise 36 is Step 8.

Exercise 37

Daniel 1:8

<u>Daniel – Uncompromising Servant</u>

Dan 1:8 - But Daniel resolved that he would not defile himself with the king's food, or with the wine that he drank. Therefore he asked the chief of the eunuchs to allow him not to defile himself. ESV

<u>Guiding Commentary</u> – Daniel was a teenager when he was taken from his home and placed into the court of Nebuchadnezzar, king of Babylon. He was placed into the training program for royal advisors, and he ought to be regarded as one of the giants of the faith. Daniel served God by serving four different kings over his lifetime. In our scripture we see the first recorded time when he stood on God's word while being asked to compromise. Another well known event was when he was instructed to only make petition to Darius, and not to any other person or god, and was thrown into the lion's den. (Daniel 6)

Daniel seemed to understand, even as a teen, that a person ought to separate themselves from the things of the world, while at the same time living in the world. The story of Daniel is the story of an uncompromising servant; he did not compromise his character and personal integrity, he lived in obedience to God, while he served four great rulers as an advisor, thereby also serving God's purposes.

How often have we compromised our personal integrity in some way, just to serve our own pleasures or to please other people or maybe even to maintain our personal image?

<u>The Exercise</u> – This exercise is meant to be done at the end of a recovery program, for example it could be part of a 12th step. And it is meant to be discussed with a personal spiritual advisor prior to starting it, and then again on completion.

Look back to pre-recovery days and write out a list of all (up to twenty) the things you did that you now know were in violation of God's instructions. Write them out as a three column list. Column one is the activity, two is the instruction that you violated and column three is a comment on whether you knew you were breaking God's word at the time. Now do the same exercise for the period you have been in recovery.

In the third part of this exercise, write a journal entry about areas you can identify in your life as areas of habitual disobedience, even though you have been through a recovery program. Write out the thoughts and feelings that go along with this, remembering that none of us ever gets it completely right; and progress, not perfection, is our objective!

Finally, write out a personal prayer asking God to give you His grace and power in being able to be an uncompromising servant as you serve your recovery fellowship or your church.

Sponsor Notes: _____

_____

_____

Useful Feeling Words:

- Grateful, Joyful, Optimistic, Happy, Glad

Useful Attitudinal Words:

- Gladness, Giving, Gratefulness, Cheerfulness, Giddy

My Pre-exercise Notes: _____

_____

_____

_____

The suggested step for Exercise 37 is Step 12.

Exercise 38

Genesis 6:8

Noah – Separately Righteous

Gen 6:8 - But Noah found favor in the eyes of the Lord. ESV

Guiding Commentary – Noah was a 10th generation descendent of Adam through the line of Seth, his grandfather was Methuselah and father was Lamech. In the days of Noah people lived for literally hundreds of years. Adam was 930, Methuselah 969 and Lamech 777 when they died. When Noah fathered his three children he was over 500 years old, and scripture says he live to be 950. When Noah received the call, described in our focus verse it is thought he was 480, and this is when he was first told about the Ark, although we can't affirm this from scripture. However scripture does tell us he was 600 when he entered the Ark, and that he preached the coming judgment for 120 years.

As we read the scriptures around the story of Noah we see some things. The population of the earth was huge. Because everyone lived a long time, it has been estimated that there may have been as many as 6 to 7 billion people in existence, about the same as the modern day world population. There was rampant sin, and only Noah was found to be righteous, one man in a population of billions! Noah was faithful to God, he preached God's message of repentance, he declared that judgment was coming and he separated himself and his family from the world.

In Christian recovery we believe we are also called. Not to the building of Arks, preaching repentance and coming severe judgment, but to the carrying of our message to others in trouble. As we have had a spiritual experience as a result of being freed from our compulsions or healed from our diseases, we are called to give back. We, just like Noah, have separated ourselves from the world, which means the behaviors and people that are associated with the reason we entered recovery, and we are to serve God in whatever way He instructs us.

The Exercise – Write first about how you used to be part of the world system around us. Describe some of your pre-recovery behaviors and how they fit right into the world culture; include some form of word picture of how you remember you felt about being "part of the action" back then. (Words like belonging, friends and acceptance might appear in this.)

During this time did you hear from a Noah type figure(s)? Write about this experience. Follow this by talking about if you felt separated, in a scriptural sense, from the world you were part of.

Now record what you believe your current calling might be, if you already know it, within your Christian recovery group. If you don't sense a calling, why do you think that might be? Talk to others that know you well about what they think your calling may be; this is in recognition that sometimes God speaks through others in our lives, particularly discuss this with your sponsor.

Sponsor Notes: _____

_____

_____

Useful Feeling Words:

- Grateful, Joyful, Optimistic, Happy, Glad

Useful Attitudinal Words:

- Gladness, Reverent, Gratefulness, Cheerfulness, Joyfulness

My Pre-exercise Notes: _____

_____

_____

_____

The suggested step for Exercise 38 is Step 12.

Exercise 39

1 Samuel 2:12, 23

<u>Eli – Indulgent Priest</u>

1 Sam 2:12, 23 - Now the sons of Eli were worthless men. They did not know the Lord. 23 - And he said to them, "Why do you do such things? For I hear of your evil dealings from all the people. ESV

<u>Guiding Commentary</u> – Eli was the high priest and judge of Israel and from scripture appears to fulfill those roles well. However he was weak and indulgent with his two sons, Hophni and Phinehas, who by virtue of their father's position were also priests. Eli allowed his sons to steal the food offered as sacrifice (1 Sam 2:12-17) where it says the sin of the young men was very great in the sight of the Lord. Eli's sons also were having sex with the women outside the tent of meeting (the Tabernacle), women who had devoted themselves to serving God. (1 Sam 2:22-25) Because of Eli's lack of discipline in his family life, which had resulted in extraordinary dysfunction in his children, God told Eli that his family was going to be cut off. (1 Sam 2:27-36) Eventually the two sons were killed in battle, the Israelites lost the Ark of the Covenant and Eli died when he heard the news, fulfilling God's promise. (1 Sam 4:1-22)

What a great example of irresponsibility and the consequences played out in dysfunctional behavior! Eli didn't take care of bringing his sons up in the admonition of the Lord, disciplining them as they were growing up so that they would be able to serve in their God-ordained role as priests. Eli allowed them to become thieves, liars, adulterers and blasphemers; the nation of Israel suffered a humiliating loss and Eli and his family died as a result of Eli's weaknesses.

That is a picture of a family in need of some recovery! For us Christians in recovery responsibility ought to be one of our themes, a song of our life that we sing each and every day. There is a basic law of life, the law of responsibility, which we all ought to memorize; <u>we are responsible for ourselves and to others</u>.

<u>The Exercise</u> – Go back to your pre-recovery days and honestly assess how well you followed that law. Start by writing about things you were responsible for but didn't take care of, giving at least one example of a negative outcome. (An

example might be that you missed work because of acting out and got fired.) Next write about things that were not your responsibility, but were someone else's, that you took care of, again detailing out at least one negative outcome. (An example here is that you bought alcohol for an alcoholic and he/she ended up with a DUI.)

Once that is done, describe any patterns you see in your life both before and after you started recovery. Lastly write about the potential long term damage you may have caused yourself and your loved ones by not taking care of the things you were responsible for. (For example, losing retirement benefits, kids need long term therapy because I partied instead of parented, or I have to divorce due to my porn habit.)

Sponsor Notes: _____

_____

_____

Useful Feeling Words:

- Ashamed, Guilty, Irresponsible, Agitated, Resigned

Useful Attitudinal Words:

- Victimhood, Sadness, Moroseness, Fearfulness, Anxious

My Pre-exercise Notes: _____

_____

_____

_____

The suggested step for Exercise 39 is Step 7.

Exercise 40

Genesis 38:24

<u>Judah – Corrupt Son</u>

Gen 38:24 - About three months later Judah was told, "Tamar your daughter-in-law has been immoral. Moreover, she is pregnant by immorality." And Judah said, "Bring her out, and let her be burned." ESV

<u>Guiding Commentary</u> – Judah was the fourth son born to Jacob, and is therefore one of the original twelve tribes of Israel. Jesus, called the "Lion of Judah" in Rev. 5:5, was to come out of this tribe. The southern kingdom formed after Israel split into two under King Rehoboam was called Judah. And Judah the man was quite controversial.

Judah is the son that persuaded his brothers to sell their younger pesky brother Joseph into slavery instead of killing him. Right after this he took off, leaving his family of origin, and went to live among the Canaanites, and took a wife from amongst them. (The full story is found in Genesis Chapter 38.) As the story unfolds we see that Judah and his new family were highly dysfunctional. Then preceding our focus verse we see that Judah's daughter-in-law tricks him into having sex with her, although he is a very willing participant, and she becomes pregnant. Then it is revealed that she has been immoral, Judah wants to put her to death (our focus verse) but she reveals that he is the father of her unborn baby(s). So he is forced to let her off. Eventually twins were born, Perez and Zerah. And Perez is part of Jesus' genealogy. (Mt 1:3)

For us in Christian recovery Judah is a study in what not to do in life. Firstly he decides to raise money by selling his brother, then he leaves the security found in his family of faith, he marries a foreign idol worshipping woman, sleeps with a family member and demonstrates self-righteousness and hypocrisy in wanting a person put to death for adultery. If we are honest, we are just like Judah, going our own way, ignoring our family of faith and making immoral choices because we have no moral anchor or guide.

<u>The Exercise</u> – Write about how you were in your pre-recovery days in the context of how Judah acted. Did you choose to ignore the morality passed on to you by

your family, and if you were a person of faith, did you ignore that too? Did you go your own way? Were you consistently making immoral choices? Describe some of these things in reasonable detail.

Now write in detail with specific examples about how you believe your recovery fellowship and maybe your church family help to protect you from immorality. Finally write a prayer, first of thanks to God for what you do have in this context, second for God to help you stay away from the immorality that you have struggled with, and finally for the truth-tellers in your life. Pray this for yourself each day for a week, and invite at least three of your truth tellers to pray it for you, also for a week.

Sponsor Notes: _____

_____

_____

Useful Feeling Words:

- Anxious, Fearful, Expectant, Encouraged, Pain

Useful Attitudinal Words:

- Thankfulness, Anxiety, Fearfulness, Ready, Hopefulness

My Pre-exercise Notes: _____

_____

_____

_____

The suggested step for Exercise 40 is Step 7.

Exercise 41

Acts 5:5

<u>Ananias – Lying Landowner</u>

Acts 5:5 - When Ananias heard these words, he fell down and breathed his last. ESV

<u>Guiding Commentary</u> – Read the whole sordid story of Ananias and his wife Sapphira in Acts 5:1-11. Here we see a couple who were seeking to obtain favor, we don't know if they thought they could bribe God or the apostles for status or approval, but it looks like it. Ananias, with the complete agreement of his wife, sold land, raised money and brought part of it to the church. That is perfectly acceptable behavior, the problem was, they lied to the Holy Spirit, and Peter confronted them about it. After Peter first confronted Ananias, the poor man dropped dead instantly. We don't know if God caused it or it was a natural death. Basically the same thing happened to Sapphira about 3 hours later. (Acts 5:11 - And great fear came upon the whole church and upon all who heard of these things. ESV)

Here is our take-away from this. It is not smart to lie to God, bad things can happen, and often do; and the rest of us ought to take notice of what happens when people knowingly and deliberately lie to the Lord who knows all. As we continue to lie to God, we begin to believe our own lies, and ultimately we are poorer for it.

Most of us would agree that everybody we know in Christian recovery that is honest would say on the record that they have lied to God. And most of us would also admit that it was never a smart thing to do. I also hope that we would all admit that lying to God, while it didn't result in our death, did produce feelings of shame and guilt when we realized our mistake. And, aren't we all glad that God loves us anyway!

<u>The Exercise</u> – This is a confessional exercise. Go back to your pre-recovery days and write out a simple admission of guilt for lying to God. Spell out the details (short version) of up to five examples of what you lied about and finish each case with a statement of remorse.

Next, do the same thing for the occasions you have lied to God after you began recovery. (Again give up to five examples.)

Finally write out a prayer for yourself having a summary confessional statement about the lies, a remorse statement, a statement of agreement with God that it is foolish to lie to Him because He knows everything, a request for God's forgiveness, another request for His help in stopping the lies and a big thank you for the love He continues to pour out on you despite your lying to Him.

Pray this each day for 5 days, and share it with somebody important in your life.

Sponsor Notes: _____

_____

_____

Useful Feeling Words:

- Ashamed, Exposed, Guilty, Reticent, Apprehensive

Useful Attitudinal Words:

- Anxious, Fearfulness, Weakness, Insecurity, Loneliness

My Pre-exercise Notes: _____

_____

_____

_____

_____

The suggested step for Exercise 41 is Step 5.

Exercise 42

1 Kings 3:9-10

<u>Solomon – Understanding Monarch</u>

1 Kings 3:9-10 - Give your servant therefore an understanding mind to govern your people, that I may discern between good and evil, for who is able to govern this your great people?" It pleased the Lord that Solomon had asked this. ESV

<u>Guiding Commentary</u> – Solomon's reign over Israel was a magnificent thing. King Solomon was a political genius, a shrewd financial manager and from a human perspective maybe the wisest man that ever lived. However he had his issues. He had 300 wives and 700 hundred concubines, imagine that! He had everything, but at the end of his life he was depressed.

In our two verses, part of a larger set (1 Kings 3:1-15), we see Solomon ask for an understanding mind, and this pleased God. In Bible folklore it is said that Solomon asked for wisdom, but this is not true. In the Hebrew Solomon uses the word "shama" which means to hear intelligently. He simply asked to be able to understand things so that he could distinguish between good and evil.

It is a common theme in Christian recovery that we struggle with understanding good and evil, so much so that we have either actively engaged in evil, or evil has stormed into our life, and it has overtaken us. There are obvious evils, such as gambling, pornography, foolish drug use and lying; and there are less obvious evils such as workaholism, perfectionism and having a critical spirit. Nevertheless, handling evil is our lot, and that is something we all have to seriously work on.

<u>The Exercise</u> – First, find a definition of evil that is biblical and that you would like to use in this exercise. Next, go back to pre-recovery days and make yourself two lists, one for evil you have done, the second for evil that has been done to you, limit yourself to a maximum of ten on each list. For each evil item, write a short description of what it was, how it impacted you or others in the short term and/or long term, including an acknowledgement if you or others benefitted from it.

Now do the same for your current life situation, but limit yourself to three of each. Catalog the evil by describing it giving as much detail as you can, the effect you believe it is having and if you are being hurt or benefiting from it.

Spend some time reflecting on what all this means to you. Write a paragraph or two about it. Then write yourself a prayer asking God to give you "shama", an understanding how to distinguish between good and evil in your own life. Pray it each day for five days. After all this discuss it with your sponsor or other spiritual adviser.

Sponsor Notes: _____

_____

_____

Useful Feeling Words:

- Overwhelmed, Struggling, Peaceful, Pessimistic, Relieved

Useful Attitudinal Words:

- Thankfulness, Resentment, Annoyed, Avoidance, Encouragement

My Pre-exercise Notes: _____

_____

_____

_____

The suggested step for Exercise 42 is Step 4.

Exercise 43

1 Kings 19:1-2

<u>Jezebel – Wickedness Personified</u>

1 Kings 19:1-2 - Ahab told Jezebel all that Elijah had done, and how he had killed all the prophets with the sword. Then Jezebel sent a messenger to Elijah, saying, "So may the gods do to me and more also, if I do not make your life as the life of one of them by this time tomorrow." ESV

<u>Guiding Commentary</u> – Jezebel was the daughter of Ethbaal, king of the Sidonians (Phoenicians) and she married King Ahab of Israel, known as the wickedest king ever to rule that nation. The marriage was a political convenience to cement trading arrangements between the great traders of Phoenicia and Ahab. When she arrived Jezebel promptly set about putting her own religions, Baal and Asherah worship, in place, and Ahab went along with it. She was also instrumental in getting the prophets of God killed off, because of course, they preached against her.

Our focus verses come from the passage right after Elijah had confronted 450 prophets of Baal and 400 prophets of Asherah on behalf of God. (Read the passage 1 Kings 18:17-40 for more on this.) God had destroyed the Baal worshipping system by having all their prophets killed, and Jezebel was hopping mad. She probably was insane, in a clinical sense, and here she threatens to kill Israel's premier prophet and God's representative.

How many of us will admit that we have had periods of personal insanity? Any decent Christian recovery program will always ask a participant to admit this, and to provide examples. How insane is it to drink oneself drunk every night, or to watch porn for hours every day, or to believe we can clean our home until it is perfect or to gamble away the kids college money or to believe that working 12 hours a day will enhance one's career? And how insane is it to wish our spouses or bosses or others close to us would disappear?

<u>The Exercise</u> – For this exercise we are going to use two definitions of insanity:

1. Doing the same thing over and over and expecting different results.

2. Doing life our own way instead of God's way.

Go back into your pre-recovery life and do an insanity inventory. Write down some of the things you did, up to 10 different examples, and explain how they were insane using both of the definitions above. Include some descriptive comments of what you feel about yourself as you go through this exercise.

Now read Romans 8:1-2 and 8:37-39. In the context of these passages, write out a prayer of thanks to God that He is freeing you from insanity through your recovery program. Pray it for yourself for 5 days, and then discuss the work with your spiritual advisor.

Sponsor Notes: _____

_____

_____

Useful Feeling Words:

- Remorse, Sorry, Guilty, Angry, Disillusioned, Upset

Useful Attitudinal Words:

- Gratefulness, Sorrowfulness, Disturbed, Remorseful, Sadness

My Pre-exercise Notes: _____

_____

_____

_____

The suggested step for Exercise 43 is Step 4.

Exercise 44

Numbers 20:12-13

<u>Moses – Unbelieving Leader</u>

Num 20:12-13 - And the Lord said to Moses and Aaron, "Because you did not believe in me, to uphold me as holy in the eyes of the people of Israel, therefore you shall not bring this assembly into the land that I have given them." These are the waters of Meribah, where the people of Israel quarreled with the Lord, and through them he showed himself holy. ESV

<u>Guiding Commentary</u> – Moses is the biggest figure found in the Jewish scriptures, which we know as the Old Testament. He was the baby placed into the Nile, the Prince of Egypt, a murderer, a runaway and he was also the person chosen by God to lead the people out of slavery and into the promised-land.

In this passage (Num 20:2-13) the Israelites had arrived at Meribah, they had run out of water, and as there were likely over a million people, this was a significant problem. Moses, who had witnessed God's amazing power, seen His ability to rescue His people, and experienced His provision, got angry with Him, and fell into disrespect and unbelief. Because of this God told Moses that he would not be allowed to bring the people into the promised-land. Notice that God had no problem with Moses being angry. The problem is that Moses, who had experienced so much with God, fell into internal unbelief with the outward result that he did not uphold God as the Holy One of Israel.

Isn't that like us in Christian recovery? We see God's power working in our lives, and the lives of those who journey through a spiritual wilderness with us. We come to our own Meribah, a place where we feel stuck and spiritually dry. We might even get angry with God, and we might also slide into internal unbelief that God is working in us, and make ourselves vulnerable to disrespectful or even contemptuous outward behaviors toward God.

<u>The Exercise</u> – Have you ever run dry in your recovery? Of course you have! In this exercise we want to identify at least one and preferably two times this has happened to us.

Think back through your recovery life, and write about what was happening in your life, and your recovery program during two dry times. Record what kinds of things you were thinking and feeling, then identify your attitudes toward recovery, your sponsor, and God. Did you slip into unbelief? Were you contemptuous or disrespectful toward God? Did you feel that He had deserted you? In a separate paragraph, write out what lessons you personally learned from this.

Finally, if you are sorry you doubted God, write out a confessional prayer of remorse about your unbelief and your negative attitudes.

Sponsor Notes: _____

_____

_____

Useful Feeling Words:

- Grateful, Encouraged, Confident, Hopeful, Optimistic

Useful Attitudinal Words:

- Gladness, Jubilant, Expectant, Appreciative, Joyfulness

My Pre-exercise Notes: _____

_____

_____

_____

_____

The suggested step for Exercise 44 is Step 11.

Exercise 45

Genesis 25:31-33

Esau – Promise Seller

Gen 25:31-33 - Jacob said, "Sell me your birthright now." Esau said, "I am about to die; of what use is a birthright to me?" Jacob said, "Swear to me now." So he swore to him and sold his birthright to Jacob. ESV

Guiding Commentary – Esau was the eldest of the twins born to Isaac and Rebekah and so would have been the one to carry on the family name and inherit God's promise to make the family a great nation. (Gen 12:1-3) He was the one who was a man's man, a hunter, Isaac's favorite. (Gen 25:28) Eventually he did become a great nation, and became the patriarchal head of the nation known as Edom, also known as Seir in scripture. Later the Edomites merged with the Ishmaelites to eventually become what we now know as the Arabs.

In the scene of our focus verses we see Esau has come in from a long day in the field and is exhausted (Gen 25:29-30) and he smells Jacob's cooking (Jacob is the other twin). He asks Jacob for some of the stew, and Jacob sensing Esau's weakness says, "Buy some with your birthright!" Esau goes for it and so gives away his family position of first son and all that means. Esau has given away something of significance for a moment's pleasure. Later (Gen 27) we see Esau tricked out of the blessing of his father by Jacob and Rebekah. Some Bible scholars believe that these two events are part of the root of bitterness that exists today, over 3500 years later, between the Arabs and Jews.

This ought to remind all of us of some recovery truisms. First, we probably all know the acronym HALT; Hungry, Angry, Lonely, Tired. We are told that it is times when those conditions exist in our life that we are most vulnerable to temptation and will make often significant mistakes. Esau was hungry and tired, and gave it all away. Second, important life altering decisions made in haste, and without due process, will often cause a massive long term relationship ripple, affecting even generations not yet born.

The Exercise – Go back through your life and identify moments that you made life-altering decisions. One-by-one write them down by describing the circumstances, the choices in front of you, your HALT condition, what your final decision was and the speed of it, and how it affected you and your closest relationships. Add anything else you think is relevant, such as did you consult others, did you consult God and how deliberate you were. Once finished, write a paragraph about any patterns you see in all these times of your life.

Now, come back to the present and write a short paragraph or two on how aware you are of times in your life when HALT is affecting you and how you handle it.

Sponsor Notes: _____

_____

_____

Useful Feeling Words:

- Upset, Concerned, Grieving, Ashamed, Guilty

Useful Attitudinal Words:

- Lost, Agitated, Foreboding, Pride, Pessimistic

My Pre-exercise Notes: _____

_____

_____

_____

_____

The suggested step for Exercise 45 is Step 4.

Exercise 46

1 Chronicles 13:9-10

Uzzah – God Violator

1 Chron 13:9-10 - And when they came to the threshing floor of Chidon, Uzzah put out his hand to take hold of the ark, for the oxen stumbled. And the anger of the Lord was kindled against Uzzah, and he struck him down because he put out his hand to the ark, and he died there before God. ESV

Guiding Commentary – Uzzah was a Levite priest who was charged with bringing the Ark of the Covenant into Jerusalem. In this story they were using a cart pulled by oxen, when God had instructed that priests they were supposed to carry the Ark on poles threaded through it. Both David the king and the priests were being disobedient.

In the story, the oxen stumbled, and Uzzah violated God by putting his hand out to steady the Ark. The Ark was where God manifested His presence to the nation of Israel at that time, and it was as if Uzzah was trying to help God do the job of taking care of Himself when he touched the Ark. Even if Uzzah had the best of intentions he still presumed that God couldn't take care of the situation. For his transgression, Uzzah was struck dead.

Isn't that so like us in recovery? We reach out to try to do in our lives, and worse than that, in the lives of those in our recovery fellowship, what God has reserved for Himself. For example, we engage in conviction (of sin, righteous and judgment, see John 16:8-11) or trying to bring rest into someone's life (Mt 11:28-30). Fortunately, God doesn't strike us down like He did poor Uzzah, but we can be sure that He does try to communicate that He does not appreciate us playing God in another person's life. He may do that directly through the Holy Spirit, or through His word, but most likely He does it through others around us who gently tell us something. Stop trying to fix other people, stop doing God's job!

The Exercise – This is an exercise that is meant to be done near the end of a formal recovery program, for example Step 10. Start by sitting with a sponsor/mentor and have him or her help you understand what "fixing" another person may look like, and how it violates God by interfering in His work. (1 Thess 5:19).

Then write about any "fixing" that you engaged in prior to recovery. Give up to five examples. Move on to the time you started recovery up to the present and first identify if you carried that old behavior of "fixing" into recovery with you, then write about some examples of where you engaged in it. Now write your version of how this violates God, if you don't agree that it does, speak to that.

Finally write a personal prayer of confession and repentance on this issue, and combine it with a prayer of request for deliverance from this sinful behavior. Pray it for yourself daily for a week.

Sponsor Notes: _____

_____

_____

Useful Feeling Words:

- Encouraged, Understood, Engaged, Optimistic, Tired

Useful Attitudinal Words:

- Vulnerable, Reticent, Resentfulness, Thankfulness, Confident

My Pre-exercise Notes: _____

_____

_____

_____

_____

The suggested step for Exercise 46 is Step 10.

Exercise 47

Judges 6:11-12

<u>Gideon – Reluctant Warrior</u>

Judg 6:11-12 - Now the angel of the Lord came and sat under the terebinth at Ophrah, which belonged to Joash the Abiezrite, while his son Gideon was beating out wheat in the winepress to hide it from the Midianites. And the angel of the Lord appeared to him and said to him, "The Lord is with you, O mighty man of valor. ESV

<u>Guiding Commentary</u> – Gideon, also known as Jerubbaal, is a mighty hero in the Jewish scriptures, but when we read the full story (Judg 6:1-8:35) we see a different Gideon, at least at first. He tested God and argued about the assignment he was given. Eventually though we see him come around. He starts off his encounters with God as a reluctant participant but eventually gets to the point where he is able to obey quickly. Sadly, after Gideon passed on at a ripe old age, the people quickly whored after the Baals again and forgot all God and his servant Gideon had done. (Judg 8:33-35)

In our focus verse we see God's calling of Gideon, a farmer, it is an assumptive calling where God is telling Gideon that he is a mighty warrior and God is with him. Notice that the scripture says "angel of the Lord" but later in verses 14. 16 and 23 the scriptures refer to the messenger of God as Lord (Yahweh). This is likely to be a pre-incarnate appearance of Christ. In the scripture after our focus verses we see Gideon testing God to make sure he is hearing right, that he is called, and that he is going to defeat the Midianites with only 300 men.

In Christian recovery we acknowledge that God is calling us out of our slavery and into freedom and healing. The 12 Steps call this Step 3. No matter what recovery program one uses, this is a fundamental calling, no lasting progress will occur until we acknowledge and accept this. In recovery we are about to do battle, just as Gideon was, and also like Gideon we are reluctant to do things God's way, because we don't have a strong belief that God can help us or that victory and freedom are possible. Just as Gideon was first called to destroy the idols in Israel, we are called to destroy the debilitating compulsive behaviors in our lives.

<u>The Exercise</u> – Write, as openly and honestly as possible, about where you are in your thinking and actions with respect to God's calling you to repent, confess, make amends and give back. Include whether you fully believe that this is a fundamental calling, a calling where you acknowledge that God is working in your life, that you have accepted it and whatever else may be relevant. Also detail out what actions you believe God is asking you to do at this early point in recovery. After doing this, pray for a week about what you have written, and ask God to reveal anything else you need to know at this point in your recovery. Add this to your work, and then discuss it with your sponsor or mentor.

Sponsor Notes: _____

_____

_____

Useful Feeling Words:

- Willing, Grateful, Apprehensive, Ready, Beaten

Useful Attitudinal Words:

- Activated, Optimistic, Cheerful, Mournful, Appreciative

My Pre-exercise Notes: _____

_____

_____

_____

_____

The suggested step for Exercise 47 is Step 3.

Exercise 48

Luke 8:41-42

Jairus – Despairing Parent

Luke 8:41-42 - And there came a man named Jairus, who was a ruler of the synagogue. And falling at Jesus' feet, he implored him to come to his house, for he had an only daughter, about twelve years of age, and she was dying. ESV

Guiding Commentary – Jairus, described here as the ruler of the synagogue, was a devout Jew, and he found himself in deep distress over the illness of his one and only child, a daughter. Nothing had worked, the physicians, prayer, beseeching God, or bargaining with God, and so he was forced to turn to a local faith healer called Jesus as a last resort. He had heard that Jesus had never failed to heal anyone who asked, and his daughter was on her death bed.

Because of these things he had to give up his traditional thinking and fatalism, all the things he had been taught as a Jewish religious leader, to go to this itinerant preacher, this man of God who preached salvation, freedom and healing. In all three versions of the story (Lk 8:40-56, Mk 5:21-43 and Mt 9:18-26) the girl was dead before Jesus arrived, and Jesus restored her to life.

Jairus reached a bottom and finally his love for his daughter overcame his cultural prejudices and he sought help from God through the source of all, Jesus. Jairus didn't know it of course, he just knew that Jesus had never failed. That is the message for us in Christian recovery. When we decide we have had enough misery, we can turn, like Jairus, to the one who will never fail us, Jesus. No matter what our situation is, drinking, drugs, sex, workaholism, perfectionism or people-pleasing, Jesus is there waiting and ready for us to say, "I can't but you can!" He wants to restore our lives, and all we have to do is give up doing everything our own way, and get out of the way!

The Exercise – For this exercise we want to look at what you have tried to do to stop acting out or to stop someone in your life from acting out. Begin by stating what you believe the problem you are dealing with might be. Then describe your own efforts to stop the problematic behaviors. You may have "white-knuckled", you may have prayed for God to take it away, or even tried to bargain with God, or possibly even wished you were dead. Describe up to 10 occasions when you tried under your own power to fix the problem, and talk about how much of your time and effort you wasted on trying to fix your own problem. Go into as much detail as your spiritual adviser suggests.

Next, describe your bottoming out process, did it take time, were you the subject of an intervention or did someone else force you to face the issue? Finally write about what the circumstances were that caused you to respond by recognizing that you were powerless over the problem or the problem people in your life.

Sponsor Notes: _____

_____

_____

Useful Feeling Words:

- Careful, Anxious, Afraid, Careless, Troubled

Useful Attitudinal Words:

- Prudence, Cautiousness, Gratitude, Shame, Guilt

My Pre-exercise Notes: _____

_____

_____

_____

_____

The suggested step for Exercise 48 is Step 1.

Exercise 49

Philippians 3:13-14

Paul – Recovering Pharisee

Phil 3:13-14 - Brothers, I do not consider that I have made it my own. But one thing I do: forgetting what lies behind and straining forward to what lies ahead, I press on toward the goal for the prize of the upward call of God in Christ Jesus. ESV

Guiding Commentary – Paul, called Saul in his pre-Christ following days, was raised to be a Pharisee of Pharisees. He was trained by the very best that Israel had to offer and most likely would end up one day as the chief priest of the nation. That destiny came to an end when he met Jesus. (Acts 9:1-22) After his conversion he became the greatest missionary the world has ever seen, and had a hand in evangelizing much of what we now call Europe.

When we read Paul's writings, maybe as much as two thirds of the New Testament, we see a man in recovery, we see recovery language; just look at Romans chapter 7 as an example. We know that all of scripture was inspired by God through the Holy Spirit, and so we know that God is a proponent of recovery. Indeed, the Bible itself is the book of recovery of the entire human race.

In our scripture above, a small sliver of what Paul wrote, we see him making three important statements, and I'm going to put them in recovery language:

- That he doesn't think he made it through his recovery program under his own power.
- That he is putting the past behind him.
- That he is continuing to work his program.

This shows us a significant mindset, one that ought to be emulated. Paul knows that it is God in him, the Holy Spirit, who has brought him out of his personal pit and into the truth. Paul knows that the past is gone, cannot be changed and is irrelevant to his future. The Paul says that he is going to continue reaching for his prize, the same one we have in Christian recovery, the prize of the upward call of Christ.

<u>The Exercise</u> – For this exercise we are going to assess these three things in our recovery program. First write your honest opinion on how much you succeeded in recovery based on your own efforts, and how much was attributable to God. Write about the tough times and what got you through them. Next write at least one paragraph about your struggles to put the past behind you, talk about the barriers you face in doing this, and how you are dealing with them. Lastly, write about what you see as the prize in your recovery, consider including references to relationships, sobriety, godly character and giving back.

Sponsor Notes: _____

_____

_____

Useful Feeling Words:

- Searching, Relaxed, Connected, Cheerful, Encouraged

Useful Attitudinal Words:

- Readiness, Optimism, Content, Vibrant, Thankfulness

My Pre-exercise Notes: _____

_____

_____

_____

_____

The suggested step for exercise 49 is step 11.

Exercise 50

1 Kings 12:6-7

<u>Rehoboam – Disregarding Newbie</u>

1 Kings 12:6-7 - Then King Rehoboam took counsel with the old men, who had stood before Solomon his father while he was yet alive, saying, "How do you advise me to answer this people?" And they said to him, "If you will be a servant to this people today and serve them, and speak good words to them when you answer them, then they will be your servants forever." But he abandoned the counsel that the old men gave him and took counsel with the young men who had grown up with him and stood before him. ESV

<u>Guiding Commentary</u> – Rehoboam was the son of Solomon who took over the powerful nation of Israel upon Solomon's death. One of Solomon's other sons, Jeroboam, came back from Israel and promised to serve Rehoboam if he would lighten the load that their father had put on the people. (Read 1 Kings 12:1-33 for a fuller picture of what happens)

In our passage above, Rehoboam does a smart thing; he goes to his father's experienced advisors and asks for their perspective. But he doesn't like what they have to say, so he goes to his personal friends, younger and less experienced, but more likely to speak things he would be able to accept. What happens next, after taking advice from his friends, is that the nation splits into two, his brother Jeroboam, promptly is made king over Israel, the northern kingdom, and Israel begins idol worship. With one choice to dismiss advice from experienced people Rehoboam destroys all that David and Solomon built up over 80 years and turns the God worshipping nation into an apostate state.

This choice, the one to ignore advice based on experience, even if we don't like the counsel given, is one all of us face in recovery, both secular or Christ-centered. So many of us, as we enter into recovery, listen to the other newbies, who are our new friends, instead of listening to the grizzly old veterans. One of the problems for newbies is the internal pressure to keep at least one foot in our old life, with the other in recovery. Inexperienced recovery practitioners will inadvertently suggest this is okay, and they will also not know or understand the new pressures that come with trying to change or stop compulsions. Veterans will spot troubles in our recovery or be able to warn us of what to expect going forward; not listening can lead to disaster.

<u>The Exercise</u> – Write a couple of pages on these two subjects. Advice I've been given on my recovery by veterans and advice I've been given by newbies (less than 6 months active recovery) and friends outside recovery. Describe the advice, then write a paragraph comparing the two, and finally state what advice you are taking, and what you are going to put aside.

Discuss the results of your exercise with your spiritual advisor.

Sponsor Notes: _____

_____

_____

Useful Feeling Words:

- Fearful, Intimidated, Sorry, Concerned, Agitated

Useful Attitudinal Words:

- Withdrawn, Resentful, Uncomfortable, Cautiousness, Sorrow

My Pre-exercise Notes: _____

_____

_____

_____

The suggested step for Exercise 50 is Step 2.

Addendum 1

Exercises by Suggested Step

21	Gen 49:1-2	Jacob - Defective Inheritor	7	44
39	1 Sam 2:12, 23	Eli - Indulgent Priest	7	80
40	Gen 38:24	Judah - Corrupt Son	7	82
11	Lk 19:8-9	Zacchaeus - Repentant Taxman	8	24
36	Philemon 10-12	Onesimus - Repentant Slave	8	74
3	Jonah 1:1-3(a)	Jonah - Disobedient Grump	9	8
28	2 Kings 20:1	Hezekiah - Prideful King	9	58
31	Hos 3:1-4	Gomer - Symbollic Whore	9	64
13	Judg 3:11-12	Othniel - Godly Protector	10	28
22	Judg 14:2-3	Samson - Sex Addict	10	46
46	1 Chron 13:9-10	Uzzah - God Violator	10	94
23	Jer 1:11-12	Jeremiah - Called Newbie	11	48
24	Job 42:1-2, 6	Job - Godly Self-Despiser	11	50
32	1 Sam 1:4-7(a)	Hannah - Faithful Intercessor	11	66
35	Ezek 24:15-16	Ezekiel - Willing Loser	11	72
44	Num 20:12-13	Moses - Unbelieving Leader	11	90
49	Phil 3:13-14	Paul - Recovering Pharisee	11	100
14	Acts 5:33-34	Gamaliel - Secret Agent	12	30
26	Mt 4:21-22	Zebedee - Sacrificing Father	12	54
27	Josh 2:3-4(a)	Rahab - Godly Prostitute	12	56
37	Dan 1:8	Daniel - Uncompromising Servant	12	76
38	Gen 6:8	Noah - Separately Righteous	12	78

Addendum 2

Exercises by Scripture Reference

30	Hos 1:2-3	Hosea - Suffering Husband	5	62
31	Hos 3:1-4	Gomer - Symbollic Whore	9	64
16	I Kings 16:29-30	Ahab - Inherited Evil	4	34
23	Jer 1:11-12	Jeremiah - Called Newbie	11	48
9	Jn 1:46-49	Nathanael - Honest Seeker	1	20
8	Jn 18:33-35	Pilate - Judgmental Blamer	4	18
19	Jn 7:50-52	Nicodemus - Truth Seeker	2	40
24	Job 42:1-2, 6	Job - Godly Self-Despiser	11	50
34	John 20:27-29	Thomas - Disbelieving Believer	3	70
3	Jonah 1:1-3(a)	Jonah - Disobedient Grump	9	8
27	Josh 2:3-4(a)	Rahab - Godly Prostitute	12	56
22	Judg 14:2-3	Samson - Sex Addict	10	46
13	Judg 3:11-12	Othniel - Godly Protector	10	28
47	Judges 6:11-12	Gideon - Reluctant Warrior	3	96
11	Lk 19:8-9	Zacchaeus - Repentant Taxman	8	24
48	Lk 8:41-42	Jairus - Despairing Parent	1	98
5	Mt 14:29-31	Peter - Doubting Rock	6	12
26	Mt 4:21-22	Zebedee - Sacrificing Father	12	54
44	Num 20:12-13	Moses - Unbelieving Leader	11	90
20	Num 20:23-24	Aaron - Approval Addict	4	42
49	Phil 3:13-14	Paul - Recovering Pharisee	11	100
36	Philemon 10-12	Onesimus - Repentant Slave	8	74

Addendum 3

List of Feeling and Attitude Words

Positive Tone/Attitude/Emotion Words

Amiable	Consoling	Friendly	Playful
Amused	Content	Happy	Pleasant
Appreciative	Dreamy	Hopeful	Proud
Authoritative	Ecstatic	Impassioned	Relaxed
Benevolent	Elated	Jovial	Reverent
Brave	Elevated	Joyful	Romantic
Calm	Encouraging	Jubilant	Soothing
Cheerful	Energetic	Lighthearted	Surprised
Cheery	Enthusiastic	Loving	Sweet
Compassionate	Excited	Optimistic	Sympathetic
Complimentary	Exuberant	Passionate	Vibrant
Confident	Fanciful	Peaceful	Whimsical

Negative Tone/Attitude/Emotion Words

Accusing	Choleric	Furious	Quarrelsome
Aggravated	Coarse	Harsh	Shameful
Agitated	Cold	Haughty	Smooth
Angry	Condemnatory	Hateful	Snooty
Apathetic	Condescending	Hurtful	Superficial
Arrogant	Contradictory	Indignant	Surly
Artificial	Critical	Inflammatory	Testy
Audacious	Desperate	Insulting	Threatening
Belligerent	Disappointed	Irritated	Tired
Bitter	Disgruntled	Manipulative	Uninterested
Boring	Disgusted	Obnoxious	Wrathful
Brash	Disinterested	Outraged	
Childish	Facetious	Passive	

Humor-Irony-Sarcasm Tone/Attitude/Emotion Words

Amused	Droll	Mock-heroic	Sardonic
Bantering	Facetious	Mocking	Satiric
Bitter	Flippant	Mock-serious	Scornful
Caustic	Giddy	Patronizing	Sharp
Comical	Humorous	Pompous	Silly
Condescending	Insolent	Quizzical	Taunting
Contemptuous	Ironic	Ribald	Teasing
Critical	Irreverent	Ridiculing	Whimsical
Cynical	Joking	Sad	Wry
Disdainful	Malicious	Sarcastic	

Sorrow-Fear-Worry Tone/Attitude/Emotion Words

Aggravated	Embarrassed	Morose	Resigned
Agitated	Fearful	Mournful	Sad
Anxious	Foreboding	Nervous	Serious
Apologetic	Gloomy	Numb	Sober
Apprehensive	Grave	Ominous	Solemn
Concerned	Hollow	Paranoid	Somber
Confused	Hopeless	Pessimistic	Staid
Dejected	Horrific	Pitiful	Upset
Depressed	Horror	Poignant	
Despairing	Melancholy	Regretful	
Disturbed	Miserable	Remorseful	

Neutral Tone/Attitude/Emotion Words

Admonitory	Dramatic	Intimate	Questioning
Allusive	Earnest	Judgmental	Reflective
Apathetic	Expectant	Learned	Reminiscent
Authoritative	Factual	Loud	Resigned
Baffled	Fervent	Lyrical	Restrained
Callous	Formal	Matter-of-fact	Seductive
Candid	Forthright	Meditative	Sentimental
Ceremonial	Frivolous	Nostalgic	Serious
Clinical	Haughty	Objective	Shocking
Consoling	Histrionic	Obsequious	Sincere
Contemplative	Humble	Patriotic	Unemotional
Conventional	Incredulous	Persuasive	Urgent
Detached	Informative	Pleading	Vexed
Didactic	Inquisitive	Pretentious	Wistful
Disbelieving	Instructive	Provocative	Zealous

This organized list is provided to help those who are working on the exercises in these books. Emotion and attitude words are very useful in helping prepare answers to questions and for mentors, sponsors, coaches and counselors in their work with those in recovery.

Addendum 4

Ten Emotional Needs

During our time in recovery we have noticed time and again a common theme running through the stories we hear. There seems to be some emotional needs that we all have in common and that are so often glaringly not met in those who live a life involving significant compulsive behaviors. This list is provided for sponsors, mentors, counselors or other spiritual guides and the individuals who use this book as an aide in working through issues. As a person works a program or walks through counseling, this list might help unlock some things for them.

These are listed in alphabetical order; different individuals need different amounts of these, and/or have different levels of deficits of these in their life.

- **Acceptance** - deliberate and ready reception with favorable positive response (Rom. 15:7)
- **Affection** - to communicate care and closeness through physical touch (Rom. 16:16)
- **Appreciation** - to communicate with words and feelings a personal gratefulness for another (1 Cor. 11:2)
- **Approval** - to think and speak well of (Rom. 14:18)
- **Attention** - to take thought of another and convey interest and support; to enter into another's world (I Cor. 12:25)
- **Comfort (empathy)** - to come alongside with word, feeling, and touch; to give consolation with tenderness (Rom. 12:15)
- **Encouragement** - to urge forward and positively persuade toward a goal (I Thess. 5:11, Heb. 10:24)
- **Respect** - to value and regard highly; to convey great worth (Phil. 2:4)
- **Security** - confidence of harmony in relationships; free from harm (Rom. 12:16a)
- **Support** - come alongside and gently help carry a load (Gal. 6:2)

Addendum 5

Exercise Record

Use this simple log sheet to keep a record of when you did an exercise and any quick thought you may have about it for your own future reference. It has been helpful to some to go back and do an exercise again a few months after doing it for the first time and comparing their answers.

	Exercise Theme	Date	Short Comment
1	Ziba - Untrustworthy Servant		
2	Michal - Condemning Wife		
3	Jonah - Disobedient Grump		
4	Uriah - Dead People-Pleaser		
5	Peter - Doubting Rock		
6	Esther - Fasting Queen		
7	Abram - Friend of God		
8	Pilate - Judgmental Blamer		
9	Nathanael - Honest Seeker		
10	Goliath - Invincible Corpse		
11	Zacchaeus - Repentant Taxman		
12	Timothy - Faithful Child		
13	Othniel - Godly Protector		
14	Gamaliel - Secret Agent		
15	Cain - First Murderer		
16	Ahab - Inherited Evil		
17	Elijah - Idol Hunter		
18	Rebekah - Conniving Trickster		
19	Nicodemus - Truth Seeker		
20	Aaron - Approval Addict		
21	Jacob - Defective Inheritor		
22	Samson - Sex Addict		
23	Jeremiah - Called Newbie		

24   Job - Godly Self-Despiser   _____ _____

25   Amnon - Family Rapist   _____ _____

26   Zebedee - Sacrificing Father   _____ _____

27   Rahab - Godly Prostitute   _____ _____

28   Hezekiah - Prideful King   _____ _____

29   Joseph - Life Saver   _____ _____

30   Hosea - Suffering Husband   _____ _____

31   Gomer - Symbollic Whore   _____ _____

32   Hannah - Faithful Intercessor   _____ _____

33   Vashti - Prideful Rebel   _____ _____

34   Thomas - Disbelieving Believer   _____ _____

35   Ezekiel - Willing Loser   _____ _____

36   Onesimus - Repentant Slave   _____ _____

37   Daniel - Uncompromising Servant   _____ _____

38   Noah - Separately Righteous   _____ _____

39   Eli - Indulgent Priest   _____ _____

40   Judah - Corrupt Son   _____ _____

41   Ananias - Lying Landowner   _____ _____

42   Solomon - Understanding Monarch   _____ _____

43   Jezebel - Wickedness Personified _____ _____

44   Moses - Unbelieving Leader   _____ _____

45   Esau - Promise Seller   _____ _____

46   Uzzah - God Violator   _____ _____

47   Gideon - Reluctant Warrior   _____ _____

48   Jairus - Despairing Parent   _____ _____

49   Paul - Recovering Pharisee   _____ _____

50   Rehoboam - Disregarding Newbie   _____ _____

Addendum 6 - Example 12 Steps

This is a list of the 12 steps for one of Merimnao's support groups, used by permission of Merimnao Healing Ministry. This particular list is from their Castimonia – Men's Sexual Purity Group, see Castimonia.org for information on them and how to contact the group.

1. **We admitted we were powerless over our addictions and compulsive behaviors, that our lives had become unmanageable.** *"I know that nothing good lives in me, that is, in my sinful nature. For I have the desire to do what is good, but I cannot carry it out."* (Romans 7:18)

2. **We came to believe that a power greater than ourselves could restore us to sanity.** *"For it is God who works in you to will and to act according to his good purpose."* (Philippians 2:13)

3. **We made a decision to turn our lives and our wills over to the care of God.** *"Humble yourselves, therefore, under God's mighty hand, that he may lift you up in due time. Cast all your anxiety on Him because He cares for you."* (1 Peter 5:6-7)

4. **We made a searching and fearless moral inventory of ourselves.** *"Let us examine our ways and test them, and let us return to the LORD."* (Lamentations 3:40)

5. **We admitted to God, to ourselves, and to another human being the exact nature of our wrongs.** *"Therefore confess your sins to each other and pray for each other so that you may be healed."* (James 5:16)

6. **We were entirely ready to have God remove all these defects of character.** *"Humble yourselves before the Lord, and he will lift you up."* (James 4:10)

7. **We humbly ask Him to remove all our shortcomings.** *"If we confess our sins, he is faithful and just and will forgive us our sins and purify us from all unrighteousness."* (1 John 1:9)

8. **We made a list of all persons we had harmed and became willing to make amends to them all.** *"Be kind and compassionate to one another, forgiving each other, just as in Christ, God forgave you."* (Ephesians 4:32)

9. **We made direct amends to such people whenever possible, except when to do so would injure them or others.** *"Be devoted to one another in brotherly love. Honor one another above yourselves. If it is possible, as far as it depends on you, live at peace with everyone."* (Romans 12:10, 18)

10. **We continued to take personal inventory and when we were wrong, promptly admitted it.** *"So, if you think you are standing firm, be careful that you don't fall!"* (1 Corinthians 10:12)

11. **We sought through prayer and meditation to improve our conscious contact with God, praying only for knowledge of His will for us and the power to carry that out.** *"Do not conform any longer to the pattern of this world, but be transformed by the renewing of your mind. Then you will be able to test and approve what God's will is – His good, pleasing, and perfect will."* (Romans 12:2)

12. **Having had a spiritual experience as the result of these steps, we try to carry this message to others and to practice these principles in all our affairs.** *"Praise be to the God and Father of our Lord Jesus Christ, the Father of compassion and the God of all comfort, who comforts us in all our troubles, so that we can comfort those in any trouble with the comfort we ourselves have received from God."* (2 Corinthians 1:3-4)

Addendum 7

The Three Books

There are three books in this series "Recovery Exercises for Christians" each having 50 written exercises for those in the world of Christian recovery to use.

1. Random Scriptures
2. Books of Wisdom
3. Characters of the Bible

Random is a set of exercises that are taken from all over the Bible. Books of Wisdom is 50 exercises taken out of the three books of wisdom, Psalms, Proverbs and Ecclesiastes. Characters is a set of 50 exercises based on the lives of real people as described in scripture.

The development of the three books occurred as we worked with sponsees on the early part of their programs, and noticed that there was a need for some scripture centered study material. This came from some core beliefs we have. First, that scripture is the infallible source for all written wisdom, given to us by God Himself for use as a guide to real life. Second, that the Bible itself is the book of recovery; it contains the story of God's work to recover the entire human race. This makes our God the God of recovery.

It is our contention that all peoples in all nations ought to consider themselves in recovery, because we believe this is true:

Rom 3:23 - For all have sinned and fall short of the glory of God. ESV

Every human has fallen short, and so all need to be recovered. We hope that these three books contribute to that happening in some people's lives.

My Notes

Use the next few pages to write out your random thoughts, individual musings, deep meditations or personal revelations. Be sure to date them for your records.

My Notes - Page 2

My Notes - Page 3

My Notes - Page 4